Birth and Death

Birth and Death

Reverend Leandra Robertshaw

Throssel Hole Press

Hexham

Northumberland

978-1-4583-5746-5
Imprint: Lulu.com

Throssel Hole Buddhist Abbey
Carrshield
Hexham
Northumberland
U.K.
NE47 8AL

Acknowledgements

All quotations from the daily scriptures used at Throssel Hole Buddhist Abbey are taken from; 'The Liturgy of the Order of Buddhist Contemplatives for the Laity', Shasta Abbey Press, (1990).

Quotations from the 'Shushōgi', and the 'Kyōjukaimon', (and commentary) are taken from; 'Zen is Eternal Life', by Rev. P.T.N.H. Jiyu-Kennett, fourth edition: Shasta Abbey Press, (1999).

The quotation on page 1, from the Angutara Nikaya is taken from; 'The Numerical Discourses of the Buddha: A Complete Translation of the Anguttara Nikaya', translated by Bhikkhu Bodhi. Wisdom Pub., (2012).

'Sitting Buddha' (2004), 'Buddha recognizes Buddha' (2010) and 'Delving' (2021), are by Reverend Daishin Morgan, and published by Throssel Hole Press.

References to the works of Simone Weil, are from; 'Attente de Dieu', (1950).

Quotations from the 'Shōbōgenzō', by Great Master Dōgen, are from; 'The Treasury of the True Dharma Eye: Zen Master Dogen's Shobo Genzo', translated by Kazuaki Tanahashi. Published by Shambala, (2013).

The quotation on page 15 by Nāgārjuna, is from; 'A Practitioner's Guide to the Middle Way', by Barry Kervin. Wisdom pub., (2019).

Dainin Katagiri is quoted on page 32, from; 'Each Moment Is the Universe: Zen and the Way of Being Time', Shambala Pub., (2009).

'Buddhism without beliefs', by Stephen Batchelor was published by Riverhead books, (1997). It is quoted on pages 80 and 87.

Sarah Maitland's 'The book of Silence', was published by Granta (2008). 'How to be alone', was published by Picador (2014).

Quotes from Ryōkan are taken from; 'One robe, one bowl', translated by John Stevens, and published by Shambala Pub., (2006.).

The quote from Tenzin Palmo on page 41, can be found in; 'Cave in the snow', by Vickie Mackenzie, which was published by Bloomsbury pub., (1998).

Alva Noë, 'Out of our heads', was published by Farrar, Straus and Giroux, (2010).

The Thomas Merton quote on page 40 is from his collected journals; 'Entering the Silence.' (Various publishers).

The quote on page 47 is from Colin McGinn, 'The Mysterious Flame: Conscious Minds in a Material World'. Published by Basic Books, (1999).

The quote on page 51 is from; 'Cultivating the Empty Field: The Silent Illumination of Zen Master Hongzhi', translated by Taigen Dan Leighton with Yi Wu, and published by Tuttle Pub., (2000).

The quote on page 71 is from; 'The Teachings of Zen Master Man Gong', translated and adapted by Zen Master Dae Kwong, Shambala pub., (2009).

The quote on page 75, from King Prasanjit is from an interview with Thich Nhat Hahn, by Melvin McLeod in 2006, published in 'Lions Roar'.

'Consciousness: an introduction' by Susan Blackmore, was published by Routledge (2010). The quote from Stephen Pinker is from; 'How the mind works'. Penguin books, (1997).

The quote from Bodhidharma on page 92 is from 'The Zen teaching of Bodhidhharma', translated by Red Pine. Published by North Point Press, (1989).

'Zen mind, Beginners mind' by Shunryu Suzuki, was published by Weatherhill, (1970).

'Deepest practice, deepest wisdom', by Kosho Uchiyama, translated by Daitsu Tom Wright and Shōhaku Okamura, quoted on page 100, was published by Wisdom Pub., (2018).

With gratitude to Rev. Master Daishin,

for all he has offered, and continues to offer to me.

Preface

It was the encouragement of my Master; Rev. Master Daishin Morgan, that nudged me into publishing this book.

I wrote these words during the time that I, and my fellow senior monks had to keep the monastery at Throssel Hole closed to visitors due to the pandemic and the dangers of rising Covid infections—it was then with trepidation that I showed Rev. Master Daishin what I had written down. Despite my fears, he graciously offered helpful suggestions, delicately put, with the result that I didn't simply shred what I had showed him.

Ever since I first met Rev. Master Daishin, somehow I have managed to trust his wisdom and wise discernment, even . though he subsequently made me wait, what seemed to me like interminable years before he finally agreed to my joining the community of Throssel monks.

I now know, without a shadow of doubt, that the consequence of having to bide my time like that led to the deep gratitude that I now have for this monastic life; a gratitude that is vast and without boundaries.

I should also like to thank Rev. Lambert Tuffrey, for his willingness to use his editing and design skills to help turn this project into a book and make these words available to others.

Contents

1.

Setting the Scene

I HAVE CHOSEN to address the question of birth and death for, (as it says in the Shushōgi); *'The most important question for all Buddhists is how to understand birth and death completely for then, should you be able to find the Buddha within birth and death, they both vanish'.*

There is a very old proverb; *'Time waits for no man'*, or as the warrior Karna said, in the Mahabharata; *'I see it now—this world is swiftly passing'.*

The Anguttara Nikaya says: *Just as one whose clothes or head had caught fire would put forth extraordinary desire, effort, zeal, enthusiasm, indefatigability, mindfulness, and clear comprehension to extinguish the fire on his clothes or head, so that person should put forth extraordinary desire, effort, zeal, enthusiasm, indefatigability, mindfulness, and clear comprehension to obtain both those wholesome qualities [of serenity and insight]'.*

Another way Great Master Dōgen puts it, (in 'Rules for Meditation') is; *'Do not waste time with this and that—you can possess the authority of Buddha. Of what use is it to merely enjoy this fleeting world? This body is transient as dew on the grass, life passes as swiftly a flash of lightning, quickly the body passes away, in a moment life is gone.'*

These words can sometimes galvanise me into practising with more gusto, but at other times the fieriness of training as if my hair were on fire doesn't fit. What fits instead (with reference to 'The Scripture of Avalokiteshvara'), is sinking into a *cool and silver lake*; sinking, sinking, sinking to the bottomlessness of its cool, cool water. That unfailingly inspires me to keep going.

This writing is a description of the path of training taken by a particular individual seeking, (as it says in the Shushōgi) to *break the chains that bind us to birth and death;* seeking indeed to find how to live as full a life as any human being can within the limits of birth and death. Another individual will have their own unique way.

What I am hoping to do in this book is to test my understanding from different perspectives, in order:

To become aware of whatever moves me beyond self-centeredness, for I believe from learnt experience that when I am not stuck in self-centeredness positive seeds are sown in my heart-mind, which are then given the environment to flourish and grow, and be nurtured so that they can be of benefit to others and to the world. (In a sense this has nothing to do with me and yet, of course, I am involved). There is an imperative to discover, through clear looking, what moves me beyond self-centeredness.

To follow the bodhisattva path and (with reference to the four Bodhisattva vows), try to keep the impossible vow to help all beings (myself included) to awaken to enlightened reality.

To find true compassion that is free of attachment. A compassion that is more than an emotional response; rather, a firm commitment founded on reality. Only then will there be a truly compassionate attitude toward others that does not change even if they, from where I am currently looking, seem to be behaving badly. What really is compassion if it is not based on the needs of others?

To keep asking the '*what*' question, as in; 'what is this Leandra-being that is no-self?' The question that leads me to wonder; 'do moments of no-self arise because the Leandra-being has let go of seeing herself as a separate being?' The question that my own Master, Reverend Master Daishin Morgan has answered in his book 'Delving', by writing that; '*my self-awareness remains intact, but its context is altered*'.

Setting the scene

2.

Death

I FIND MYSELF more and more often returning to the question of birth and death—small wonder perhaps, now that I am in my mid 80's and have a long life behind me.

It is a paradox that the more we take on board, and are in touch with our responses to even the smallest changes in our environment (both external and internal), the more we also come across our internal stability which is not stirred by conditions. That stability is the Unborn, the fundamental nature of being. It is beyond pain, *for here there is no suffering*, (as it says in 'The Scripture of Great Wisdom'). Alertness to the transient, brings together awareness and memory. The French philosopher Simone Weil in her book; 'Waiting for God', said that it is the power of attention that points to eternity. She said that if we pay attention closely enough we will come to know the transcendent, for it lies in the centre of the human heart and mind. She wanted to appreciate, understand and weep with the suffering of the world.

Death

So each morning, as I awake to a new day I see myself as somehow a new person in spite of there being nothing fundamentally different: my arthritic legs are still arthritic, but there are subtle changes too and it feels right to not go down the path of wondering why the pain is more or less intense than on other mornings. If I were to do that, my whole-being would be narrowed and confined to the perception of pain. Then I would be a person looking for a remedy rather than one accepting circumstances as they are at that moment.

We *are* going to die. We *are always* dying. Death is *now* as each moment passes irrevocably.

So what then is a reliable refuge? This question takes me to a depth I will never be able to fathom. It takes me to the question; *what am I?* This is a depth I must explore quickly, for (as it says in 'Rules for Meditation'); '*life passes as swiftly as a flash of lightning*'. There is an urgency to this.

When we have been practising wholeheartedly for decades, it is not surprising that our awareness and scrutiny leads us to engage with the onset of old age, disease and our inevitable death. A fine trainee I know was once on the verge of moving from his current house to another one that could be adapted for his increasing frailty and ill health. He wrote the following; '*I have found a buyer for this house but haven't found one to move to. So I know where I am leaving from, but not where I am going to.*'

Taking his predicament more deeply the trainee had looked into the meaning of the word 'dwell', which though it does mean to live in a place, can also mean to live in a particular way and in addition could mean to remain for a time. This had brought up for him the thought of living in *whatever* house for the time being, and of dwelling in *this body/mind* for the time being. This life, he had realised and this "I" is just for the time being.

For me this brought to mind Dōgen's expression; *reality manifests itself for the time being as an ordinary person*, a paraphrase from the chapter called 'Uji', or 'Being-time', from the 'Shōbōgenzō'. Everything is in this moment. Awakened practice can only happen in this present moment. As Dōgen also taught in this chapter; '*Although the Dharma might seem as if it were somewhere else far away, it is the time right now*'.

I was and continue to be grateful for the time spent training with the writer, grateful for the years we have been practising together even though I live in a monastery and he lives the householder's life. What in particular resonates for me is that both of us in our own ways are sensing what remains to be done as we approach the end of life and are deepening our trust in *what is*, without having an idea of what's next.

This sense of trusting reminds me of another member of our congregation, called Brian who came to be in a hospice towards the end of his life. I am reminded of his 'excitement', that he would soon have the opportunity of dying and would 'know' what death is, and what comes next.

Death

The final stages of Brian's death though were hard to witness. He was in immense pain; he tore out the tubes infiltrating his body, he rattled the cage of his bed. In the midst of witnessing this, I turned to a poem by the American poet Mary Oliver, called; 'When Death Comes'. It ends thus; *'I don't want to end up simply having visited this world'*.

My sense that Brian had not simply visited this world was reinforced at his funeral in Gateshead. The chapel was packed with his mates who worked for the company where Brian was foreman. So many men indeed that the majority were not able to get into the chapel itself, but stood outside.

When it comes time for dying we can take nothing with us. If we can truly acknowledge this we can cease from causing ourselves unnecessary suffering by desperately trying to hold on to anything—even the sense of what we are.

Are *you* afraid of dying?

If you are, is that partly because you don't know what will happen after you die?

Here are a few possibilities:

Energy is neither created nor destroyed. Just as the elements of our body; carbon, nitrogen and calcium were passed through innumerable bodies before our birth, so too will they be recycled when we die, to become part of building many new bodies, from plants to people. In the same way psychic energy, (relating to, or denoting faculties or phenomena that are apparently inexplicable by natural laws), is also recycled. Phenomena relating to the soul, mind or spirit, such as anger; compassion; confusion and clarity will all continue on and be part of a new constructed self.

Once we accept the fact that body, heart, and mind are inseparable, we can become free of the struggle to make the mind, spirit, or soul remain active after the body stops working. Everything is interconnected, and after death no part of us stays as it was. You may go to heaven, paradise, or hell, or be reborn into this world with the deepest, unknowable part of yourself, but it is extremely unlikely that any part of your body or mind will be brought with you as it now is. This realization may initially cause a great deal of angst. However, we all need to start with the acceptance of its truth. Only after we fully face, take up our abode in, and make peace with the existential reality, can we become liberated. As it says in 'The Scripture of Great Wisdom'; '*For here there is no suffering. In the mind of the Bosatsu who is truly one with Wisdom Great the obstacles dissolve.*'

With the constant updates in the media about the number of coronavirus deaths and with the constant updates too about the rise, then fall, then rise again of infections as new variants appear, we cannot avoid thinking about death. It does not help in the face of this to cling to doctrines or to the soothing words of others.

They don't ultimately cut the mustard. Instead, we must, as it were jump out of bed as soon as the alarm clock rings. Don't just lie there. How else, but with such a bright willingness can you even face death, which always comes?

Am *I* afraid?

I used to hope it was merely the process of dying that frightened me. Once in a dharma interview, (where monks speak privately with their Abbot), I was invited to call death to be there in front of me, rather than lurking behind my shoulder. What excellent advice that was, because following it allowed me to be at one with my death, to truly look death in the face and thus to begin to realise that death is not an object separate from myself—death outside me, so to speak, and me inside. Instead, life and death are one reality: as I took my first living breath, it was, at the same time the first breath of dying. We *are* all dying all the time.

'*If I say I am not afraid of dying, am I deluding myself?*' This is a question it behoves me to keep asking. Yet these days when I do ask myself this question, it doesn't feel like I am deluded when I answer myself, that I am not afraid of dying. After all, I do know other aspects of fear, so I do know what it is to be afraid.

Even so, though I do know that I can be at one with ordinary fears, I do need also to take on board the possibility that fear of death is the ultimate fear; one that is too big or too opaque for me to be easily at one with. Nobody else can take away this concern for me. So what's to be done? My response is to investigate with all the integrity I have at my disposal, with all the longing to know reality. To explore what it is to be a human being who is both a lonely individual and at the same time inextricably the whole world, utterly connected with everything else. It seems worth all of us asking ourselves what we wish for in life given the personal being we see ourselves as, and also asking what we wish for our world from which we cannot separate ourselves. It is delusion to think there can be any separation.

Scrutinize carefully—don't try to dodge your moral, preceptual nature that shrivels when, for instance, you say that which is untrue. This is for your sake as much as for the sake of others. Don't let yourself get away with fudging things in the hope that it will make them easier to accept. Unless we kill ourselves death is not a decision we make, therefore let us decide to live life as fully engaged as we can by being open to everything, able to hold everything in a spacious stillness, a radiant calmness. We are thus learning to cradle both the immense sorrow and wondrousness of life, cradle both at the same time. We are learning to be with pain and pleasure, joy and sorrow, with hearts fully open. Hearts that are intact even when it feels they have been irretrievably broken.

How about in old age approaching our inevitable death with a youthful curiosity as well as with courage and a willingness to keep growing? This will require attentiveness and working with our hardwired emotions; seeing from moment to moment that we always have a choice to react more intelligently and kindly to others, and to resist hurting them because of our confusion and self-centeredness. We may still be at the stage of aspiring bodhisattvas, (beings who help others), yet it is important to acknowledge that our aspiration to be of service remains unwavering in spite of the mistakes we make. It helps to cut off any desire to justify our selfish behaviour immediately we become aware of an unskilful habitual response.

'Do we have a mountain of karma to clear up before we die, in order not to be reborn?' Here is a question some ask. We do undoubtedly have to deal with what we have done. We are responsible for cleaning up the karma we received at birth, and if we work at this we will pass on a welcome gift to future beings. Surely, it is deeply saddening to know we have been continuing acts of body, speech and mind time after time, even though they make us ashamed and lead us to suffer as much as the suffering they have inflicted on those we have hurt. Yet, with sincere practice the landscape can change and the task of cleansing is never over for we see at deeper and deeper levels the harm we have been doing to ourselves and to others. We peel off yet another skin of the onion.

We take responsibility for all the mistakes we have made, rather than slithering away and hoping to excuse ourselves by blaming others or blaming unfortunate circumstances that we try to insist were not of our making. This will be an amazingly beautiful process of growth and maturation. We are uncovering insight into the Samsaric web we have been weaving through our thoughts and actions and the ensuing karmic consequences, both good and bad that have endlessly rippled out. This spiritual maturation is a background from which compassion flows naturally.

HOW TO DEAL WITH THE LOSS OF A DEARLY BELOVED BEING

Penetrate the loss, express it as eloquently as you are able and then let go. Don't deny death and grief, allow them to flow through you. There is for all of us unimaginable loss ahead including the possible end of human life on earth. How will we bear the grief ahead, will we allow grief to make it harder to act? We may want to find a 'cure' for grief. Rather, allow the possibility that grief too is a Buddha. It can be a wonderful teacher. We are invited to be stained by grief, made holy by grief. Know that grief is a form of love and then as we go on without our beloved, love isn't diminished. We are transformed by our loss. A genuine love acknowledges our debt to our beloved and we can be alone with dignity.

We are all coming to realise what life and death are. The understanding of today is not the understanding of tomorrow and yet nothing is missing in the understanding of today. Without fail this coming to realise, assists us in being with, what in 'The Scripture of Great Wisdom' is described thus; *'all things...are neither born nor do they wholly die'*. I had a profound sense of this on the first anniversary of the death of a fellow monk, particularly of the words *nor do they wholly die*, as for me she had not wholly died, her presence continued, and continues to be vividly here, now. Our disagreements, though sometimes forcibly expressed, had never divided us. I recalled recently, for example that at one point she had been certain that a particular person should not be ordained as a monk. Eventually that person was ordained, but then later chose to leave. Their time here as part of the novitiate was not a mistake as I know that it has helped them to find another way of offering to others. So it turns out that neither my fellow monk, nor I was completely right nor completely wrong. I find myself wishing we could discuss this again. Yet there is no need to, for in a mysterious way we keep up the conversation.

Some of what we say about birth and death can lose its punch if we recite something so regularly that we hardly notice what we are saying. For example, the shaving verse monks recite each week;

> *'Now as we are being shaved, let us pray that*
> *We may leave behind worldly desires for eternity;*
> *After all, neither birth nor death exist.'*

Such a verse has a tremendous power, yet from frequent repetition we can fail to see it.

The wave and water analogy that is often used in Buddhism has helped me to see there are two dimensions to life and we touch both. In the historical dimension there are certificates for birth and death—this is the wave that has a beginning and an end. However, in the dimension of immediacy, the flowing world of water, there is no beginning and no end. As our great spiritual ancestor, Nāgārjuna said in a work called; 'The Fundamental Wisdom of the Middle Way';

Birth and Death

'Before something is born, did it exist?
Something already present can't be born.
To be born means from nothing you became
something, from no one you became someone.
But nothing can be born from nothing.'

I have tried reciting these words as if working with a kōan, so that whenever during a day I recall them, I say them to myself without expecting a comprehensible answer.

I continue to *long* to understand birth and death completely and that longing is taken to my sitting place, for on my cushion there is a deep trust in the efficacy of zazen to reveal the riddle of the no-birth of all things. To find a calm peace in the midst of thoughts such as these is the demonstration that life is a continuum. In this very moment *now* anything can happen. While it is the case that to speak of happening implies duration, what is required is to carefully observe what changes, as duration unfolds. We can become more alert to one thought ending and another not yet begun and rest in that space which could be described as the unchanging heart of this very moment.

Although I am often uneasy when I talk about the present moment, I also sense that dropping the notion of the present moment altogether is avoiding what is important. For now, the conclusion I am stuck with is that the present moment holds the recent past together with the immediate future. I think I am suggesting that maybe we discover more about being a human being by dropping any concern of defining the present moment, or for that matter of defining any concept. Rather the direction of concern might more profitably be engagement with a deeper awareness of the consequences of living one way rather than another.

Nirvana seems to me at present to mean extinction, extinction, extinction. Extinction of all notions and concepts; such as birth/death, being/non-being, coming/going. Nirvana is the ultimate dimension of life; a state of coolness, of peace, of joy, of profound serenity. It is not a state you attain after you die for you can reach it right now. As Dōgen says in the chapter called 'Gyōji', or 'Continuous Practice', from the 'Shōbōgenzō'; *'On the great road of Buddha ancestors there is always unsurpassable practice continuous and sustained. It forms the circle of the way and is never cut off. Between aspiration, practice, enlightenment and nirvana there is not a moment's gap; continuous practice is the circle of the way.'*

In the 'Avatamsaka Sutra' we are assured that in touching one moment with deep awareness, we touch all moments. If you can live one moment deeply that moment contains all the past and all the future. Touching nirvana frees us from many worries; things that upset us no longer feel that important and a day later we can look back in some puzzlement at how stressed we allowed ourselves to become.

I remind myself that I never know anything with unwavering certainty. Acknowledging this pushes me further off balance and into unknown territory. Then great joy arises because it is evident that life and death are always sufficient and my befuddlement is no hindrance. As we step into the unknown the door to death opens. Let us step through it with curiosity instead of fear.

Death

3.

Who, or what am I?

I HAD BEEN REFLECTING on the question of whether we remain the same person when our intellectual ability diminishes. When somebody is steadily declining into dementia, do the changes, including their personality, mean they are no longer the same person? If not, then who or what are they? How important is memory in defining who we are for it seems to fade as we age: we forget words and probably a former ability to use a rich and nuanced vocabulary diminishes. Correct grammar may remain but in telling a story we can feel we can't engage an audience as we used to be able to do. Does any of this matter? Does it decrease our value as a human being? There are those old people whom others describe admiringly as being as "sharp as a needle" i.e. really on the money intellectually. Are they more valuable people than those who are dementing?

In asking *who am I?* I know it is more than asking about my personality. The question is deeper than that. However, exploring personality might help somewhat in answering the question—and it might not. So is this leading anywhere useful? Might it help if, for instance, I acknowledge, with a wry smile, my propensity to energetically and enthusiastically engage with whatever situation reveals itself? Recently, this led to falling flat on my face as, in going through a door I tripped over a step. It was as if the two elements of body-mind were out of sync and the willing mind rushed ahead of the ageing body. I recognise what could be described as a rather 'over-enthusiastic' engagement with life. This seems to be a habitual aspect of being Leandra that is not diminishing with age. It was useful to acknowledge this to myself in order to see if it was a way of ignoring the ageing process. So then I wondered if our 'personality' becomes more entrenched as we age. Do we become more set in our ways? Less able to change and adapt?

In meditation the next morning after the fall, further questions arose about personality. Do we sometimes define others in terms of their attributes, their personality? Can personality change, or is it hard-wired by upbringing and genetic inheritance? As I sat in the Zendo, there arose a strong sense that my 'personality' had been partly assigned to me by significant adults from as early as I can remember. That I had been assigned a mixture of what others wanted me to be (family, teachers, friends etc.), or that I had been given labels that didn't really seem to fit. For instance, was I really shy? Or was it, as felt from the inside, that I was I most at peace when there was no expectation that speech was the method of communicating? There had always seemed to be many other ways of communicating that I learnt from being around animals or peers. I recalled an excruciating incident when allowed out of boarding school for the day with an aunt. She took me to watch a polo match, knowing that my father was a polo player. It had been a nice choice, but one spoiled by her insisting that I go and ask a group of strangers what time it was. This she saw as a way of curing my "shyness";

But…but I know what time it is Aunt Iris.

No matter, simply do as I say!

Such occasions of what felt like adult intrusion must have stayed with me, even though I was no longer conscious of them and the influence they had had on my adult life. Now reflecting back I see that when I became a mother, my hope for the children was that they would discover for themselves how best to live their lives. I trusted them to do so and tried not to needlessly interfere. Looking back, I see that this was not a conscious, deliberate decision. What I wanted to offer was unwavering love and trust in them to find good ways of being alive. For some parents giving this kind of care comes naturally and I was blessed in being such a parent. I give thanks for this. Such loving care is not needy, not greedy, not self-indulgent and not neurotic. Such profound love is not erotic, sentimental, not attached. Real love seems to be marked by a deep and transformative feeling of care and sadness.

These days I am often sad and welcome sadness as reality which is offering a truth that I can open my heart and hands to gather up. Sadness seems to come about through taking responsibility for all the mistakes I have made, rather than blaming circumstances or other people. Although often sad I am also joyful and at peace. I love life, do not fear my death, and am so grateful to this Sōtō Zen tradition into which I unwittingly stumbled. The joy is seeing how huge, completely unobstructed and how precious everything is. When I am conscious of joy I realise it is because at that moment I am not caught up in any emotional or physical pain—whether mine or others. I have also laid down worry, even the huge concerns of what we humans have done and continue to do to this beautiful world. If this were not so, joy would be obscured, and I would have lost the important essence of the enormity of joy when not obstructed by unending suffering. How precious everything is when for a moment the view widens so that resentment, bitterness, grudges and fears are not obscuring the view. Greed, hatred and delusion may never totally end, but there are respites from their poisonous influence.

Returning to questioning whether the concept of personality is useful for spiritual life, I ask myself about the individual 'personalities' in a community of monks. We live so cheek-by-jowl the temptation to feel irritated and impatient can be strong. What then? Because of my sincere vow to keep the Precepts I know without doubt that I must find a way of letting go of how I would like people to be. It is ludicrous, sad and divisive if I grumble to myself, or worse grumble to another about somebody else. Here right in front of my nose is an opportunity to practice letting go of personal preferences, and of how I wish others would behave. If I feel stressed by living in community then I ask whose fault that is. Surely it is nobody's fault, not even mine.

How much grief we can avoid if we lay aside competitiveness, even competitiveness with our former selves.

When I first came to live at Throssel I found myself wondering what the heck I had done, for here I was living with people I would previously not have chosen to spend time with, and here I was leaving behind those I loved and felt in tune with. Now it is different, and I feel gratitude that I have the blessing of living in this community. It was my naivety that played a part in that earlier assessment of monks, for I had come with the crazy belief that all the monks were perfect human beings whose example I would try to emulate. Why else would I have come and set aside a life that was for many reasons good enough? I hadn't taken heed of the advice in the 'Sandōkai'; *'Here born we clutch at things and then compound delusion later on by following ideals.'*

Who, or what am I?

4.

Emotions

I FEEL IMPELLED to say something about emotions as they are part of our practice that cannot be ignored because if they are not deeply seen through, they can cause untold difficulties for oneself and for other people. It is a natural mistake to think we understand emotions; what they are and how we come to feel them, but research suggests we are often at odds with their reality. There is, for instance, the danger of over-egging emotions as a way of justifying behaviour that is more usefully seen in the context of greed, hatred and delusion. There is value to taking on board how looped together emotions and thoughts are—a thought in a flash becomes an emotion, and an emotion can reveal the thought with which it is inextricably bound.

The classical view of emotions remains compelling, despite the evidence to the contrary, precisely because it is intuitive. It also provides reassuring answers to deep, fundamental questions like: Are you responsible for your actions when you get emotional? Do strong feelings ever justify bad behaviour? How accurate is your assessment of what another person is feeling?

Research with facial EMG (electromyography), shows that muscle movements of our faces cannot reliably indicate when someone is angry, sad or fearful. Fear, for example, does not have a single expression, rather is a diverse population of facial movements that vary from one situation to the next and from one person to another. This resonates with what practice encourages us to realise; the complexity and the richness of how humans behave in relation to each other. When we firmly plant ourselves in reality and not in some imagined or wished-for world, we see more clearly the ever-changing circumstances life offers. We are more likely to notice differences in how others respond, for instance when angry—some fume, some cry, others are quiet and cunning, some withdraw. Even small changes, such as leaning forward with arms crossed or leaning back, alter an angry person's physiological response.

Context is crucial, such aspects as body language vary with the social situation people are in at the time, or how different cultures behave in expressing emotion, and so on. On different occasions, in different contexts, within the same individual and across different individuals the same felt emotion will lead to different responses. Variation, not uniformity, is the norm. An emotion is not a thing but a category of instances and any emotional category has tremendous variety, probably governed by whatever prepares your body best for action in a particular situation. Variation is not an error but normal and even desirable.

As Darwin said, we are a population of unique members who differ one from another.

Your past experiences arising from, for instance, direct encounters, social media, daily news, films, books, works of art, give meaning to your present sensations. Yet, the entire process of construction is invisible to you. In every waking moment you are faced with ambiguous noisy information from your eyes, ears, nose and other sensory organs. Your brain uses past experiences to construct an hypothesis and compares it to the cacophony arising from your senses. What we see, hear, touch and smell are reproductions of what we decide the world is, not solely reactions to it. Your brain makes best guesses so invisibly and automatically at what the world is, that vision, hearing and your other senses seem like reflexes rather than the constructions they actually are. We temporarily lose sight of our existence as an entity composed of the dynamic activities of our senses.

What about sensation from inside the body? These sensations have no objective psychological meaning until your concepts enter the picture. Here is a nice example; a judge in the courtroom has a gut feeling the defendant cannot be trusted, when actually she, (the judge) is merely hungry!

Best not to speak of perceiving someone's emotion 'accurately'. Perceptions exist within the perceiver. Emotions are not built-in, waiting to be revealed. They are made by us. We are architects of our own experience, thus it behoves us to try to give up deeply ingrained ways of thinking, and courageously allow certainty to turn into doubt. We are deluded if we want to excuse our behaviour as being due to a strong emotion arising. This means it won't do, for instance, to justify our angry behaviour by claiming it is due to our being at the mercy of a powerful emotion. If we are tempted to excuse ourselves in this manner, we are behaving un-preceptually. We are choosing to ignore the Precept 'Do not Be Angry'. Anger arises for us all at times, but we need to practice being with it and not taking our anger out on another being or object.

Here is Dōgen's commentary on this Precept in the 'Kyōjukaimon'; *There is no retiring, no going, no Truth, no lie; there is a brilliant sea of clouds, there is a dignified sea of clouds'*. Rev. Master Jiyu, in her commentary adds; *Just there is that going on which causes us to see unclearly; but if we truly look, if we look with care, we will see that the true and beautiful sky is shining behind the clouds; we may see the Lord of the House. No matter how angry the person is who is with us, we may see in him, too, the Lord if we are truly looking, if your own ego is out of the way and, in seeing the Lord in him, he can see the Lord in us. The depth of the ocean is still even when there is a great storm upon its surface; thus should we be when there is anger, knowing that nothing whatsoever can touch the Truth.'*

Controlling our behaviour is up to us, for we are the architects of our emotions. Your river of feelings might feel like it is flowing over you, but actually you are the river's source. We like to think we're reacting to what's actually happening in the world, but really the brain is drawing on our deep backlog of experience and memory, constructing what it believes to be our reality, cross-referencing with incoming sense data from our heart, lungs, metabolism, immune system and adjusting as needed. This defies common sense because almost always we act on predictions our brain is making about what's going to happen next; we are not reacting to experience as it unfolds.

Emotions don't happen to you; they are made by your brain as you need them. The more you know about emotions, the more precisely the brain can construct them, so you will feel and act in ways that are very specific to the situation. We can broaden our experiences today to predict differently tomorrow. We can broaden our horizons to have more flexibility in constructing our predictions before the heat of the moment leads to actions we come to regret. Even our firmest intuitions can be horribly wrong and lead us astray. Because persistent uncertainty is very, very hard on a human nervous system we turn to concepts as tools for making emotions.

Emotions

5.

Loneliness and Solitude

LONELINESS

IN CHOOSING THE MIDDLE WAY, there is no fixed reference point to which we can defer. The mind with no fixed reference point does not fixate or grasp. I wonder if it is too much to ask though, for us to *live* without that reference point. For to live with no reference point would be to challenge our deep seated habitual response to the world—our wanting to make things work out one way or the other. It could feel so terrifying, to live in this way—being unable to go left or right…surely we would die! We could feel utterly alone with no handhold to use to get out of the deep darkness of despair. But by being still, patient and trusting, the result would be a dawning on us that we already know that going to left or to right, or believing that there is always a right or a wrong has never really changed anything. That scrambling for security has never brought us anything but momentary relief; a relief like shifting our position when sitting in meditation, only to find any relief from discomfort to be so very fleeting.

Becoming unstuck from any deep-seated habitual response requires us to be brave. For instance, we are called to come to terms with acknowledging that not only do we seek resolution of our difficulties but we expect that resolution, we feel we deserve it. When we have the courage to look with integrity and honesty at the deeply buried motives in us that cause harm, we are shining a light on them. I call this *beginning to see the bright light of the Middle Way appearing through the clouds of delusion*. I know without doubt, and yet also inexplicably, that there is the Middle Way waiting wide open for me to find. This seems to require sensing my utter loneliness and trusting that it will not decimate me if I sit within it and face it head on, thus feeling what I feel, not running to left or right, not falling into judging whether I am deluded or sane.

WAYS OF BEING WITH LONELINESS:

Dainin Katagiri Rōshi once said; *'One can be lonely and not tossed away by it.'* Here though are some thoughts from my own experience, about how to be at peace and find freedom within loneliness.

The first is to watch how quickly your habits become stories and then how quickly your stories become your excuses. I am slowly learning to stop reiterating what I am apt to consider my very important story line and see how ephemeral it actually is and how everybody else has their own story line too, which is neither less nor more important than mine. Not making your stories your excuses will help you become quicker at noticing when you are beginning to wander into the realm of desire. Desire burns at the core of life and is usually complicated. One spiritual solution to desire may for some be to try to flee from it. This is unlikely to be helpful; rather, the way through seems to lie in non-attachment, thus transcending the body-mind and its deeply-rutted, habitual ways of responding. Do not lie to yourself by trying to convince yourself you have no desires. Rather, see that what you desire can fade and change.

One of my children when he was young used to decide in advance what he would spend his pocket money on, but he would wait a while because he knew from past experience that his wanting this or that changed. This was a lesson he taught me! If we obstinately cling to a certain desire it will cause much conflict in our heart-mind.

When the passion and sorrow—all the vulnerability that links me to the world—feels too much to bear, I recognise the temptation to look for ways to soothe my loneliness. But I find that, for instance seeking comfort in food and drink, is pointless. What is needed is to realise I have set myself the task of preparing to leave home, to become homeless and thus to relate directly with the way things are. The way to be with loneliness when it begins to feel unbearable, is not to give up and try to solve the biting feelings but to sit within them. Thus I am letting go of the crazy idea that I am in control of how life is, and am instead turning towards trusting that there is truly nothing that needs controlling or solving.

Passion and sorrow have their place in my life, in the life of all things in this world.

Let's move on to considering how to be content when alone. Perhaps, this is easier as we age and begin to understand that to be lonely is the human condition. Loneliness is a reminder that we know love. Within the sadness of being alone there is a kind of fullness, a fullness of the heart. The sadness comes from the awareness of the transience of all things, yet alongside it there can be the joy and appreciation of their truth and beauty. The older we get, the greater the opportunity to let go of relationships, of objects. Friends die, objects break.

When we have nothing, we have nothing to lose. If you find value, even joy, in losing things, you might also be lucky enough to lose who you thought you were. We can learn to give away what we have discovered as easily as we can give away what we have been given. This brings to mind these words from the 'Sandōkai'; *Within all light is darkness but explained it cannot be by darkness that one-sided is alone. In darkness there is light but, here again, by light one-sided it is not explained. Light goes with darkness.'*

Thus we can find ease, contentment, and the feeling of being unrestricted, peaceful and free. Thus we are able to respond appropriately with wisdom and loving kindness and without judgment to our world as it is, as it constantly changes. We can learn to navigate circumstances with agility and responsiveness instead of reactiveness.

Birth and Death

We are offered a wonderful opportunity as we get older to keep dancing to the tunes of the world with dignity and grace.

We are learning to be with not-having, not-knowing, without a reference point, without a hand to hold. Then we can choose between freaking out, or settling in. I often regard contentment as a synonym for loneliness as I begin to realise there is no escape from loneliness. Just *be* lonely with no alternatives, content to be right here with the mood and texture of what's happening. Then gratitude appears for the preciousness of being alone and content.

Another useful tip is to avoid unnecessary activities. When loneliness seems unbearable the temptation is to keep ourselves busy, thus avoiding the pain loneliness can bring on. As Sara Maitland writes in 'A Book of Silence'; *Rigorous busyness...can easily be an evasion of or a defence against the silence and one's own fragility in the face of it.* 'Or as Ryōkan said; *If you want to find the meaning, stop chasing after so many things'.*

I have found it takes a certain discipline to be at ease with loneliness. I need to come back gently, at every opportunity, to the present moment. There I find a willingness to sit still, to just be there, alone. When I acknowledge my fundamental aloneness wherever I am, whatever I am doing, and that there is nothing anywhere to hold on to, this leads to the possibility of finding a completely unfabricated state of being, a seeing in a fresh, open way; a realising of the profundity of the unresolved issues of my life.

Finally, there is looking with compassion and humour at what I am. Solitude's grace allows loneliness to come and go, without pushing it away or clinging to it. No constant 'self' that's experiencing any of this. Yet, I do not hold myself aloof from life—that is impossible. Loneliness is not always about being alone, but about feeling out of step with others. For me this can occur when, for instance, I am with friends or family and they are drinking alcohol. The more loudly they enjoy themselves the more isolated I feel.

Norman Fischer, a former Abbot at San Francisco Zen Center talks about *ineffable aloneness,* which he feels describes the sense that aloneness can be too great, or too extreme to be expressed in words, too sacred to be uttered, something both completely alone and completely connected. An example is bowing to another; there is love, respect and gratitude, and there is the space between us. So there is both connection and emptiness. I turn yet again to the 'Sandōkai'; *'each sense gate and its object all together enter thus in mutual relations, and yet stand apart in a uniqueness of their own - depending and non-depending both.'* Alone and connected, both are true. How? Maybe it is because both are the same thing.

There is the intimacy of connection with everything, and yet each of us is a universe on our own. This translates for me as both a longing for solitude, and a longing for connection with others. I find I can simultaneously ride both these horses when I receive what is currently foremost, without wishing for the other. There is no point in trying to choose, for it is not in my control, rather something transcendent is at work: the universe in its totality and the mystery of this particular mind and heart. I bow in gratitude and humility.

Moments of such knowing of emptiness are up-cheering because it is not all about me, and of course I am involved. It helps to know that all meetings end in partings. This is the reality of connection; both together and apart, for there is emptiness too—an experience of emptiness that is an experience of non-duality. Non-duality sees no boundary or distinction among various aspects and values of things. There is no duality because the momentum of awakening is already present within circumstances as they are. This means all of us are both radically <u>in</u>dependent, and at the same time radically <u>inter</u>dependent.

WHAT IS MEANINGFUL

Language imprisons us and words are at the same time the way out. Words are needed and yet the meaning is not in the words. So what's to be done except stumble on in the dark, reaching out, trusting, trying to understand who or what I am, and who or what we all are as individual beings. A helpful companion on this path is compassion—compassion for myself and for others, for I truly know we all are doing the best we can. What also helps on this path is to realise that my ignorance solidifies a false reality. Ignorance suggests that I and my world are separate, enduring, solid things.

What unanticipated joy there can be then, in those solid things falling apart, for the blessing of such inevitable times is that they leave us feeling groundless and uncertain. At first this may feel most unwelcome—but look again at the opportunities that unfold from this: For instance, we come to appreciate in a new way the suffering that ensues when we are holding on to a relationship we should let go of; or when we have publicly made a fool of ourselves. Or when we have revealed to others our mendacity, and in our embarrassment mixed with fear we have tried to deny reality and tried to rebuild our ego as if nothing had happened. This of course expands our suffering, because the consequences of our behaviour cannot be avoided, and importantly, we have, through timidity and fear, thrown away an opportunity to learn from our mistakes.

When we know the blessings that lie in things falling apart, we can realise that we need to go back to the beginning and start again. There; we can be at peace in the groundlessness and the uncertainty, but no peace will be found in trying to escape the discomfort. Let us learn to rest in the vast space of reality—open and awake. Then our true nature is revealed beyond the ups' and downs' of life.

SOLITUDE

Sara Maitland, in the introduction to her book; 'How to be Alone,' suggests that; *'when you find it difficult to concentrate; constant interruptions, the demands of others, your own busy-ness and sociability, endless contacts and conversations make it impossible to focus.'* This may make you realise that you need to find some solitude. How you respond to it though will differ depending on whether you are really seeking solitude, or actually doing all you can to avoid it.

Being alone can be rare in our lives, and the rarer it becomes the more potential there is for us to learn from it. When you are alone, try experimenting with avoiding reading and writing. See what happens when the talking stops and you even turn off your mobile phone and close down your laptop. What happens when you try going out in nature, to see if that makes being alone less demanding for you? (You might find you are at one with the natural world in a more intense way than you have previously been). Take note of how time passes, and of any changes in how you relate to the world as the day wears on. Does the experience compare to your expectations? You have the opportunity to see what it is like to be you, alone. Ask yourself if there a difference for you between solitude and loneliness.

William Wordsworth in 'The Prelude' wrote;

> *When from our better selves we have too long*
> *Been parted by the hurrying world, and droop,*
> *Sick of its business, of its pleasures tired,*
> *How gracious, how benign, is Solitude.'*

This solitude is something sought of course. When solitude is forced on us, by imprisoned solitary confinement, bereavement or the breakdown of intimate relationships, then naturally it can bring up fear and the sense of being overwhelmed by circumstances we have not sought, and would at all costs have tried to avoid. Being solitary by choice however, calls to me, and I find that it doesn't necessarily mean I need to live alone. The call can be answered living within a community. I can find, and make room regularly for solitude. I can find a way to be alone within the rhythm of my ordinary daily life, where I can relax and expand, and pay attention to both my interior and exterior life. Then I can come to realise that I have found a way of pushing out my boundaries, so to speak, and miraculously as I do so, those boundaries seem to move further out of themselves without my conscious intervention. The spaciousness I find has expanded, and in that space there is more of the world waiting for me. Solitude and silence seem to be vehicles for transcendence. They enhance and develop self-awareness. As Thomas Merton said; *'All men need solitude in their lives to enable the deep inner voice of their own true self to be heard.'*

Sara Maitland singles out two renowned hermits: Antony the Great, (AD 251 - 356) and Tenzin Palmo, the British-born Tibetan Buddhist nun.

Antony the Great, (AD 251 - 356) was an early Christian hermit living mainly in the Eastern desert of Egypt. He was the founder and father of desert monasticism and had a major influence on the development of Christianity. He attracted many followers. The focus of his practice was on inner silence. For the Desert Fathers though, hospitality and kindness were more important than keeping their ascetic practices. One of the hermits said; *'Take care to be silent. Empty your mind.'* I would not be surprised to hear this from a contemporary Zen teacher.

Tenzin Palmo is a Tibetan Buddhist nun, renowned for the telling of her story in the book; 'Cave in the Snow'. She spent 12 years in the cave, and when asked to reflect on how that had been, said; *'Certain days were marvellous and there were others of extreme unease when I wished I could do something other than sitting and meditating'.* When I myself have been on 3-month retreats and found them very challenging, I wasn't even restricting myself to sitting and meditating!

Henry Thoreau wrote in his book 'Walden', about the enhanced sense of self he found in going to live alone in a wood in Connecticut for two years; *'I went to the woods because I wished to live deliberately, to front only the essential facts of life, and see if I could not learn what it had to teach, and not, when I came to die, discover that I had not lived.'*

I have found for myself when out walking, that there is a difference in whether I do so with others or on my own. Walking on my own intensifies how I experience things through the senses, both physically and emotionally. Walking with another, in silence, does not dissipate the experience in the same way. But walking and talking is a different matter; it is as if I am overloading the senses and communicating verbally has dissipated my awareness of the environment in which I am moving.

Contemplation, or reverie is a useful way of understanding patterns in our internal life and seeing where we set boundaries. It can be helpful at the end of each day to review your practice, as this can be a tool for understanding how and why those moments come of feeling joyfully bound to the whole earth, to the whole universe. You may get hints of why the social presence of others distracts or reconstructs our sense of a core self.

6.

Consciousness

IS CONSCIOUSNESS a useful concept in your practice? Dōgen advises us in 'Rules for Meditation'; *'Control Mind function, will, consciousness, memory, perception and understanding; you must not strive thus to become Buddha.'*

What am I striving for is perhaps a place of freedom which I might call the Buddha realm, somewhere I can dwell where I absolutely know that the Leandra-me is the world, and where this infinitesimal part is also the vast, vast whole. How miraculous those times are when we can experience the *beyondness*, the utter spaciousness; the immovable in the midst of the passage of time, change and decay. This miracle can happen again and again because each occurrence, though different is inseparable from any other occurrence. This is about non-duality; an understanding of 'not one' and 'not two'.

Any action, however small or large affects self and other; cause brings forth effect. The seeming dualistic perspective of

Consciousness

Buddhist ethics—that is to say good and bad, right and wrong—is in reality based on non-duality. What Dōgen described in 'Genjōkōan', (from the 'Shōbōgenzō'), as *actualising the fundamental point;* is the extremely subtle, mysterious unfolding of nirvana within the life of change and decay; the 'Unborn'; the indestructible. We all can come to realise this, by going into and maintaining the deep awareness that is sometimes experienced in zazen, and in daily activities conducted in the meditative state of body-and-mind as one.

A simple approach to being conscious that Pema Chödrön recommends in her writings, is to practice noticing whatever we appreciate. We can take note of even the most ordinary of things. And Alva Noë, an American philosopher, poses an interesting thought too; *'Consciousness is not something that happens in us. It is something we do.'* (From his book 'Out of our heads'). This resonates with me, in that I notice I can go about my life, (including times of formal sitting) seeming to be there, and yet not engaged. Rather, I am so distracted, I could not even say what was distracting me from being there. But once again noticing this disengaged 'self' wandering in the realm-less realms, I am again conscious; it is as Noe says, being conscious is something that I do.

At the heart of Buddhist practice is cultivating an attentive mind with astute capacities for observing the self. Practising with dedication and vigour, we can become more capable of clear perceiving, and also be more humble about what we miss; of seeing what our own particular limitations are. We become more aware of the many causes of any action.

If you decide to investigate the concept of consciousness to see if it could be helpful in your Buddhist practice, here is a question you can ask: *is it worth becoming better at staying conscious?* To help to answer this, take note of how long it is before you realise that you are no longer really engaged with where you are and what you are. Another useful question might be to ask whether you might have deliberately turned away from current circumstances because they felt too overwhelming. Is there the possibility that at the time of the turning away, you may not have been conscious of having done so? It is difficult to backtrack through these meditative processes, as if in a court of law, and perhaps it is too tricky. But none the less, trying could help in answering the vital question; *what is this,* and again, maybe questioning yourself offers an opportunity to be with what frightens you, something that you haven't been able to acknowledge before.

Even if we all start at different levels of consciousness surely we all can become more adept at staying conscious throughout our daily life. I have found that if there is something that has been troubling me and I feel its presence throughout waking hours but keep turning away, then it is likely to reappear as a dream in an often bizarre extreme form that cannot be denied or avoided. So I wonder if the more I am aware when awake of being conscious the more I will be enabled to understand why sometimes I choose to become 'unconscious'. For being conscious means you have to feel what you feel, which often means feeling vulnerable and raw.

Consciousness

Try asking yourself: *am I conscious now?* Try doing this as many times a day as you remember to do so. You can ask the question while doing things: reading, writing, going to the toilet, washing up, eating, cleaning your teeth, etc. This is what I meant by asking if what is described as consciousness stands up to your experience.

What of selective attention? We may believe multi-tasking is to be admired and sought after, but in reality we can only be conscious of one thing at a time—even if the switch to something else is so rapid we think we are multi-tasking and thus doing more than one thing at a time. Take care with false pride.

Also consider that your experience, your understanding of the world and how we best navigate it, might be completely impenetrable to anyone else. You can try to tell somebody else what it is like for you to live in the world, but even as you struggle to do so, you might well find that your words never quite capture what it is like for you. We are the same species and yet so different from each other. Even if you are convinced that you know when you are conscious it is hard to tell another person how and why you know. This may be so because we each have our own private experience of the world that is un-shareable. Even when we are convinced we are aware of things going on around us, aware of our inner states and thoughts, it might be that we are inhabiting such a private world of awareness that it is too hard to tell another person something of what it is to be you, when you can't even describe it to yourself. I can't, for example, even convince myself that I can find a real answer to the question; *what is this?*

Birth and Death

The philosopher Colin McGinn wrote; *'the more we struggle over the puzzlement of what consciousness is, the more tightly we feel trapped in perplexity. I am grateful for all that thrashing and wriggling.'*

Struggling with the question *what is this*, may well change your sense of self. This can be darn uncomfortable. The once solid boundaries between the real and the unreal, between self and other, between humans and other animals, between you and the world, begin to look less solid. Your certainties about the world out there, or ways of knowing it, seem less tenable. You may even begin to doubt your own existence.

As I explore such doubts, what I am asking about is the deep, deep interconnection between all things. A sense of, or a 'knowing', in a way that defies definition. It might it be that our intelligence is not well designed for understanding consciousness, after all, questions about the nature of consciousness are intimately bound up with those about the nature of self. Always it seems as though there must be someone *having* the experience; that there can't be *experience* without an *experiencer*. Always it seems as if our experiencing 'self' feels itself to be at the centre of everything we are conscious of, at a given time, and that this self seems to be continuous from one moment to the next—i.e. it apparently has both continuity and unity.

Dōgen describes this situation eloquently and profoundly in a chapter called; 'Uji', or 'Being-time', from the 'Shōbōgenzō'; *'The zazen of even one person at one moment imperceptibly accords with all things and fully resonates through all time. Thus, in the past, future, and present of the limitless universe, this zazen carries on the Buddha's transformation endlessly and timelessly. Each moment of zazen is equally the wholeness of practice, equally the wholeness of realisation.'*

Ask yourselves, as I do, why questioning like this might be of value spiritually. Personally, I become less sure of who, or what I am as questions appear of themselves to demand consideration. I take on board that it is useful to keep turning my attention to whatever it is that is having the experience, and I come to doubt as a result, that we can ever really feel or see, an *experiencer* as something distinct from the experienced world.

WHAT IS THE UNCONSCIOUS?

Sometimes remaining un-conscious of some aspects of being human is a way of hiding from the challenge of investigating what we really are. It can be a way of hiding from something that we have never been courageous enough to thoroughly investigate. We can doubt our ability to bear consciously investigating what is terrifying for us, for we want such horrors to remain hidden from our sight. It is possible, however, to shine a healing light into the murky depths of our being; to look *into* what we have unwittingly chosen to try to keep hidden in our unconscious. And it may also be that sometimes nature's remedy to relieve extreme physical and mental pain, is to have us remain unconscious of it.

7.

Learning from All Living Things

WHEN I CONSCIOUSLY TAKE NOTE of, for instance, the garden outside the window, nothing is ever quite the same as it was last time I looked, listened, and felt. There is always a renewed joy in the vibrancy of the scene. Each season has its typical weather, and yet each day in each season, each minute even is not the same. There are different birds on the bird feeder, the trees are in full leaf or showing the pattern of bare branches; there is snow on the ground, or there is the green, green of a freshly mown lawn. The wind is moving the trees in a wild dance, or now and then there is no more than the gentle tremble of branches. What delight!

Recently out on a walk I was drawn by sound to stop and look.

Dark pink abundance of wild rose bush
Enticing fragrance
Bumble bee and human both drawn to the untainted
Frenzied buzzing gathering pollen

Totally single minded
Was he even aware of the entranced human observing.

Do you think your pet dog, or cat is conscious? Or the birds singing from the tree tops? Perhaps you believe that the cows gathered at the fence to stare at you are conscious, but earthworms are not. If I say something is conscious; for example, the deer in the Cleugh that catches my attention because I look up aware that I am being watched, then I can fall into imagining that what is going on in the deer's brain is it considering what sort of being I am—whether, for instance, I threaten it in any way. Then I am brought up short by acknowledging that I don't really know what another human being is thinking, so it is stretching things too far to assume I know what a different species of animal is thinking. However, if I were a deer stalker I would be likely to have studied their behaviour so intimately I could more reasonably claim to know what they are thinking, and what their next move might be.

I have a black golden-eyed cat called 'Dakini', (*sky dancer*). She is an important part of my life. Her presence in my life is precious because we all want someone, some being, to love. Maybe she is not as attached to me as I would like to imagine. Her seeming attachment is probably due to my being the one who regularly feeds her and shares a warm bed for her to sleep on! But I can't know. I do know, however, that we humans are tempted to read too much of ourselves into what we think is going on in an animal's mind. Nonetheless, there is a sense of intimacy between Dakini and me that is about entering each other's space/time and how attentive we are at observing each other. This occurs in both directions and if it is ignored there can be friction.

Much of her day and night is spent out of my sight and hearing. Hers' is another life beside my own, being fully lived. I can't assume to know what 'intimacy' might be for Dakini; does it even compute as having any relevance to the life she is living? Any speculation on my part is likely to reflect my own projections, my anthropomorphism. From a Buddhist perspective, intimacy is a quality of mind—a willingness to be present with what is going on with full physical, mental and emotional attention, free of interrupting barriers of self. When Dakini brings in a mouse at night and wakes me with her excited, turbulent cat talk, how can I not be there—physically, emotionally and cognitively—even when I try to pull the pillow over my head, and go back to sleep, hoping or trying to convince myself that whatever the messy fallout it can wait till morning?

How does the mind influence the tone of any encounter? The great twelfth century Chinese Master, Hongzhi said; *'If you feel a shadow of a hair's gap, nothing will be received'*. Whereas, what I seem to be saying is; *if only I could feel a shadow of a hair's gap, I could go to sleep again!* I know Dakini is just being her hunting-cat self, and yet I am tempted to impute all sorts of things to her behaviour; I can't help but feel she is wanting to share the excitement of catching a mouse with me, a mouse which she will then devour!

In my life with Dakini, the dimensions of our relationship expand as I spend more time observing her habits, and as we adjust to each other's routines. I must admit though, that I can let selfishness get in there by mumbling to myself that *I* am the one doing more of the adjusting. Perhaps this is an important reason for not forgetting the value of investigating consciousness and how that process can deepen our practice. What I am struggling to describe is the terrain of seeing aspects such as 'like' and 'dislike', or the making of unwarranted assumptions about another being's behaviour; as well as the over and under estimation of how my behaviour affects another being. It is well worth investigating such a fertile field for spiritual maturation.

What living with Dakini has taught me is that when one, even for a fleeting moment, perceives clearly the rich complexity and vitality of another being's life, one tastes the delicious wish for its life to continue to unfold in the best way possible. It is a moment in which there is the opportunity to practice non-dual intimacy; a meeting of the "other" in its very suchness. Examining the barriers to intimate encounter can be a fruitful practice as part of the spiritual path. I have found again and again that when I am willing to let go of whatever past difficult interactions there may have been, and take the seeming risk of being open to another person; then a 'space' appears where we both can find richness and harmony.

The joy of intimacy, however fleeting it may be, can be so unexpectedly deep and genuine that one finds again and again the willingness to approach what had seemed like a minefield of unconscious attitudes in order to engage the other more fully. This is only if we come with open hearts, minds and hands however;

only if we can come with no ulterior motives, for it is easy to come to the other wanting to be liked or thought well of. If we can even put down the wish that we could engage more fully and without envy; then inevitably we *do* engage more fully and more authentically. Meeting the other in their 'suchness', opens the heart to exquisite beauty, yet also to suffering, for there is no free lunch 'spiritually' speaking. Getting only what we imagine is the positive from an engaging with the other, without what we are inclined to label as the negative, is impossible because the positive and the negative are always intimately intertwined. What an important teaching this is of how to become less self-centered.

I have spun out so many words about learning from all living things because such *alongside-living* brings me back to my first encounter with the great mystery at the centre of the universe. I will call it the 'Unborn'. Such first encounters with the ineffable often occur when we are very young, when we are too young to find words to even try to express what has happened—not to anybody else and certainly not to grown-ups. Before now, it had never occurred to me to do so—it had never occurred to me to be something worth doing. Or maybe it was something I had always felt too embarrassed to do, but:

Back then, at the time of this first encounter all those years ago, I felt as if I was in love with everything. I felt as if I was in love with the smells; the sounds; the sense of how the earth and the sky presented themselves on that hot, dusty African afternoon. It was as if all of this love I felt was contained in concentric circles that included, in the more distant circles, human noises as people worked, talked and sung together, and then other circles beyond that which contained the sounds of animals, of birds, of livestock and domesticated animals.

Nowadays, I would say that I had felt, if only for a moment, truly at one with everything.

8.

Practice

THERE IS SO MUCH IN SŌTŌ ZEN that has transformed my life and it seems good to single out certain practices that have been, and are deeply important in how my life as a Buddhist monk has evolved. These are; Zazen, the Precepts and Scriptures. I assume they are valued by all of us. And there are other areas which I have felt pushed to investigate too, one of which is whether there is a place for psychotherapy in our practice.

ZAZEN

Meditation is the core and heart of our practice. It is the essence of our lives. The real power of meditation is that it enables us to shift our perspective, and enables right view. We stop fighting with our emotions as a result. Basically, we stop *doing*, rather we learn to simply *be*. If we feel daily life keeps pointing out that we are flawed beings, (with the result that we never feel good enough), then this is a very challenging practice as we feel there is always something missing and we have to make up for it by trying harder, or doing more. What helps me is to return again to the essence of Dōgen's teaching, that 'training and enlightenment are one' because we all have the nature of a Buddha from the beginning. *'All you have to do is cease from erudition, withdraw within and reflect upon yourself. Should you be able to cast off body and mind naturally, the Buddha Mind will immediately manifest itself; if you want to find it quickly, you should start at once'.* (From; 'Rules for Meditation').

Zazen helps to dissolve fixation on yourself or any result you are hoping to gain from just sitting. If you sit in zazen in order to achieve something, it is to miss the wonder of it. We have to let go of any idea of the path as a journey from a state of delusion to one of enlightenment. Rather, what zazen offers is a means of learning to see 'grasping' and thus to learn a non-grasping attitude. It encourages us to reflect on not having a solid identity. We observe ourselves moment after moment, seeing that our bodily sensations, our thoughts, our emotions are constantly changing. Reflection on our constant *changeableness*, without judgment or expectation encourages a brighter, truer awareness. We are no longer looking for results but practising without hope of anything beyond right now. We are allowing ourselves to be content, grounded and at peace.

Meditation has a healing power, for as we sit we can release our fear, transform our unskilful responses toward others and accept any unwanted situations we perceive ourselves to be in. We are both discovering and uncovering our kindest selves. As we sit we get in touch with our physicality. Here, by contrast is an illustration of *losing* touch with our bodies. It is a quote from James

Birth and Death

Joyce's short story collection; 'The Dubliners', where he describes a character, Mr. Duffy as; *'living his life at a little distance from his body, regarding his own acts with a doubtful side-glance'.* Let us not live at any distance, however small, from our bodies.

Some people start a period of formal meditation by paying attention to the body—what is called a body-scan. The advice is to keep in touch with your physical being, and return to it when you lose the plot in meditation and are in a dreamy state; perhaps, for instance, replaying a recent conversation with someone, or resurrecting fragments of a movie you have been watching. This helps us keep a sharp eye on sensations, thoughts and feelings as they occur. Don't assess them though, simply acknowledge them and let them pass, for; *'meditation is just sitting with no deliberate thought,'* ('Rules for Meditation'). This attention can be harder and more subtle than you might at first suppose.

In Zazen there is no way you can go wrong, wherever you find yourself, wherever feelings, thoughts, sensations take you. It is a state in which you can be anybody and anywhere. Bring in as much gentleness as you can. Trust the simple instructions you have been given. The technique is already precise; it has both structure and form. Sit trusting that form, with warmth and gentleness. That is how we can awaken to bodhicitta, the mind of awakening; an awakening that is necessarily accompanied by the falling away of belief in an inherently existing self. Just relax. Relax your shoulders, stomach, heart and mind. Have you ever tried this when preparing for sleep? Try it, as it may offer something special to you; somehow it may obviate any tendency you have to try to get Zazen right. There is no right and wrong about Zazen.

When we meditate there is nothing *more* in the world, for it is the universe calling to itself and the universe responding. Our Buddha nature is to respond, because Buddha nature is our life and the life of everything. In meditating regularly, stability and equanimity gradually evolve as we inquire deeply into the nature of what it is to be ourselves. Whatever changes, IT is enough.

KEEPING THE PRECEPTS

To keep returning to the Precepts is essential, for we are never going to be perfect beings. Breakages of the Precepts continue, however hard we try to keep them and we all too easily fail to keep our vow to 'Do Only Good'. However, don't fall into despair as a result, look with care, and you will see that any un-preceptual behaviour of body, speech and mind is increasingly happening at a subtler and subtler level. We are deepening our practice. Do not doubt that; do not look down on, or look askance at your training. Remember your wish to practice the Buddha Way—trust and have confidence in the power of this wish. We have been taught the value of working for a time with a particular Precept that we are having difficulty in keeping, for then we will find that doing so affects not only this particular Precept but also our ability to keep all of the Precepts.

Ask yourself, for instance, if you are going to allow yourself to continue for the rest of your life talking against others? It is not for instance, a valid excuse to talk against others by believing that someone's behaviour needs putting a stop to because it surely affects more people than you. Desist in judging others, rather look with bright awareness at the probability that talking against anybody due to whatever they appear to have done doesn't soothe the heart, and it may well create a schism or clique in the Sangha; the precious community that surrounds us. See when you are watering the roots of 'like' and 'dislike', because 'doing good for others' means doing good for all beings. It is *you* who are doing the watering of the seeds of discrimination and thereby causing disharmony in the precious Sangha. Not only that, but in doing the watering, you are encouraging the temptation to try to drag others into your behaviour so that you don't feel so bad at knowingly breaking the Precept of 'not talking against others'.

If we don't acknowledge cause and effect we will find it nigh on impossible to fulfill our sincerely made vow to keep the Precepts. Training encourages us time after time to look as clearly as we can, to not ignore those pinpricks of disappointment in our behaviour that we sometimes feel, and to vow yet again to 'Cease from Evil', 'Do Only Good' and 'Do Good for Others', (The three Pure Precepts).

There are three levels of the Precepts:

The first level is the literal level where we slavishly try to follow the Precepts as if they are rules set in stone. However, we soon begin to see how this does not work out in life where we have to make difficult decisions about whether a certain action, such as do not kill, leads to consequences that cause more death. Are we prepared to take on the karma of having killed in order to save many lives? Wisdom is needed to guide us.

The second level is compassion. We recognize the complexity of the living network of causality which is endlessly complicated. Our human ideas cannot encompass it. Precepts will be broken at times for the greater good. Then we need to be guided by compassion and wisdom. We turn to our heart which is the love for all beings.

The third level is the level of the ultimate. At this level the Precepts cannot be broken, or kept, for they—like all that is—are empty of any identifiable self. Knowing this we can follow the Precepts with a wide and flexible heart.

There are threads of behaviour that have become deeply ingrained between self and other, deeply ingrained over the years of training together. Slowly, slowly these threads can untangle, but due to 'habit energy' they can loop round again and if we are not really on the ball spiritually, we can stumble over the loops. A wise Master recently described them as 'imps'. We each have our own particular 'imps', our own particular Samsaric feedback loops. Accepting this, there is a sadness that arises in me which is both personal and not personal. I bow in gratitude as the sadness arises, as I am being offered the opportunity to take responsibility for all the mistakes I have made, and continue to make, in spite of what seems to be my longing to do better. Surely, to not blame myself, circumstances, or other people, is the pathway of growth and maturation. Surely it leads to a deepening insight into the samsaric web I am weaving through my feelings, thoughts and actions. Surely thus, I see more clearly the karmic consequences that ripple on endlessly.

Our kōans keep revealing themselves again and again which alerts us to the realisation they are not yet totally converted. As Rev. Master Jiyu said, the highest kōans are the Precepts. Our attempts to live a moral life in a world such as this one is what makes the kōan appear naturally in daily life. The Precepts are more than morality, rather they are a doorway to profound religious understanding. They help us find the life of Buddha that *is always increasing in brilliance* and not to kill it in ourselves or in others. When we can refrain from killing Buddha in all the little acts of daily life, goodness will take care of itself. There is a generosity of response that does not depend on rules and regulations. We forget the small self and its self-centered focus on what it feels it needs. Perhaps what the small self feels is what it wants, rather than what it needs.

When the small self is set aside, grace is freely given. We are transformed without seeking for transformation and probably without necessarily seeing it. Others find us much more worth knowing. We become poised and cheerful, able to mix with all others. We are not behaving in an artificial way that is designed to impress others. There is no affectation here because we behave naturally and within the joy of so doing we are also wise and serene. For there is *the going on, going on, going on, always becoming Buddha.* Be quietly optimistic that your resolve and vow to change will dissolve the fetters. Remind yourself that all beings have intuitive knowledge of the Buddha nature. This is what Reverend Master Jiyu called the fifth law of the universe.

As celebrant at a Spiritual Direction ceremony recently, the familiar anxiety about whether I would be able to hear the 'real question' behind the question each monk asked, drained away and I stood upright and at peace surrounded by all our ancestors who that morning seemed to me more than merely the names in the ancestral line. It was clear that they had not wholly died because they were there with us. We and they have never been separated. '*All the Buddhas True of present, past and future they ARE all*', as it says in; 'The Scripture of Great Wisdom'.

BENEFITING FROM THE SCRIPTURES

Although I deeply value all our Scriptures, at present I am drawn to talk about Avalokiteshvara (Kanzeon), the bodhisattva of compassion. So I turn to; 'The Scripture of Great Wisdom', 'The Scripture of Avalokiteshvara Bodhisattva', and 'The Litany of the Great Compassionate One' for inspiration.

I ask myself what 'The Scripture of Avalokiteshvara Bodhisattva' means for me at this point of training. How about all those miraculous things she does? Though I enjoy the poetry, at the same time, with a more analytical aspect of thought, I can find them far-fetched, and I don't resonate with them in the way I used to do. But then I look again, inspired to investigate the real meaning at the heart of this scripture, and when I do all those 'magical' solutions (to dangers and problems) no longer trouble me. Rather, I am pushed to call on the sense of wisdom and compassion within this body and mind:

There is a Kanzeon within each and every one of us. Kanzeon listens to the cries of the world; the rush and roar from beginningless time, the sounds of suffering, the current of pain that flows without ceasing. As neophyte bodhisattvas we willingly join the current of pain, we vow not to forsake beings caught in distress, and our vow helps us overcome any longing to leave this world of pain. Our willingness helps us choose instead to flow within the current of pain; to perceive the suffering and respond as best we can. Thus we are on the path of overcoming the unwillingness to face our pain and the pain of other beings; the unwillingness to exist within this suffering world.

In the morning, be one with Avalokiteshvara and the deepest
wisdom of the heart.
In the evening be one with Avalokiteshvara and the deepest
wisdom of the heart.

Suffering is boundless and immeasurable. I have begun to realise though, that it doesn't stand in opposition to joy. The first noble truth that the Buddha taught is that suffering exists; dukkha's remit ranges from un-satisfactoriness all the way to intense pain and distress. We can't get around the fact of suffering, but we can come to realise that suffering is empty, and ungraspable; that it has no edges. We can welcome it as an invitation to see our true nature, and thus become a bodhisattva for all. In accepting *any* situation we can know we are protected, and that no matter what happens, evil will not prevail. One's body may be destroyed, but one's heart is safe. Joy abounds. I am at peace and alive. As Reverend Daishin Morgan wrote in 'Buddha Recognises Buddha'; *'A faith born of daily experience shows that there is a sufficiency to be found within whatever happens'.*

Avalokiteshvara responds to an infinitude of circumstances by acquiring new qualities, putting on new robes, accepting new names, and adopting different genders (whether male, female or gender-less). In the face of changes, she gracefully adapts. Perfectly at ease despite the gigantic, impossible seeming vow to save all beings, she loosens bonds of self-fixation by putting others first. With lowered eyelids she looks inward into her own mind, and downward to witness the lamentations of the world.

Suffering takes many forms, and many resources are needed to combat suffering. Kanzeon is sometimes depicted holding a willow branch which signifies resilience, for it is able to bend in the fierce storms of disasters without being broken. Sometimes Kanzeon is shown with a thousand arms and hands each with an open eye at its centre, thus pointing to her constant awareness. At other times Kanzeon is a warrior-like figure armed with a multitude of weapons; this can remind us of the fierce aspect of compassion which we call upon to protect and guard us. One thing is for sure; if we run from suffering, harden our hearts, turn away from pain, deny life and live in fear, rather than opening our hearts toward suffering, we lose the direct path to transformation and liberation.

Recently the community watched a biographical film of Nelson Mandela's life made after he had been released from Robben Island prison. It showed that he had never let himself be bullied by the guards, instead he had taken an interest in their lives and problems. Throughout his life he always wanted to understand people, and why they took the stance they did in life. For instance, once he had been freed and was negotiating with his old enemy, the Afrikaner National Party, he amazed them by showing that he had studied Afrikaner history. He knew that Afrikaners had suffered at the hands of the British in the past, and asked why they couldn't understand that black South Africans were suffering in the same way as they had suffered. Here was a quite extraordinary man who always tried to make sense of other people's behaviour and was never unable to forgive another. In my eyes, he exemplified love, compassion and wisdom. He was a person called Nelson Mandela and he was not separate from anything else.

For any of us to discover an awakened heart within ourselves it is crucial not to idealize or romanticise compassion. Compassion is not a quality that comes and goes; it is not a divine gift. Compassion simply grows out of our willingness to meet pain, rather than flee from it. No one can build walls around their hearts that are invulnerable to being breached by life's blows. Diving deeply within to nurture courage, balance, patience and wisdom, we are naturally enabled to care and to love. We will be connected to countless beings, even those we may never meet. They may be living unimaginably dreadful lives, and in a way that is probably beyond comprehension, yet we are in touch with their pain. Compassion flows on because it is not our compassion.

Ask yourself how much you feel your heart can encompass. This will help you inch closer to realising that there are no limits, especially when you begin to understand that compassion is not a state but a way of engaging with this fragile, unpredictable world. Our capacities to cause suffering as well as to heal suffering live side by side within us. We can vow to offer healing rather than causing schisms that divide one from other.

Be willing to endlessly continue to make such a vow, even when there are times we break the vow. We learn from such falls from grace. We pick ourselves up and try again. True compassion is not forged at a distance from pain, but in its fires. We may long to fix pain but we need to put this longing aside and concentrate on finding the commitment to stay connected and listen deeply. We can become a fearless presence for another person by being wholeheartedly receptive. How fortunate we are to have the Sangha; to have spiritual friendships.

Awareness opens our hearts and minds to distress that previously only glanced off the surface of our consciousness. Each cry is a plea to be received. Remain present when you want to flee. Learn to accept the presence of what is, however ghastly or terrifying it may feel. Through acceptance one can better sense what to do, so never hesitate to do that which you know to be needed. I try to remind myself that compassion is not a quality that comes and goes, rather it embraces what we all are. Looking at myself I sometimes worry that I am not really compassionate enough or wise enough to help others, let alone myself. I find some consolation in reading again what is written on the back of my small kesa, (the reminder of the Precepts that monks wear with their day robes); '*Compassion flies free responding to need and homeless Leandra casts off*'. Then I simply get on doing the best I can. In spite of my delusive behaviour I know I do find stillness within homelessness.

'*O that my monk's robes were wide enough to gather up all the suffering in this floating world*'. (A saying of Ryōkan). I turn to such sentiments when I need inspiration, when I am feeling lost and disheartened. I repeat to myself the kesa verse;

'*How great and wondrous are the clothes of enlightenment, formless and embracing every treasure; I wish to unfold the Buddha's teaching that I may help all living things.*'

I sense that this profound wish to unfold the Buddha's teaching does help all living things; our kesas *are* wide enough to gather up all suffering. We and all other beings are treasured by the Buddha and his teaching.

The Buddha is said to have given this advice: *search the whole world and find no one deserved your love and compassion more than yourself.*

Compassion's enemy is attachment, for it leads us to resist what is, and insist that life be other than it is. To see a loved one suffer can feel unbearable. In our most intimate relationships love and fear grow simultaneously. Genuine compassion makes no distinction between self and other, thus if we feel our own suffering is unbearable, how can we bear the suffering of others whom we dearly love?

I used to work as a psychotherapist and sometimes with people who had been sexually abused. It was harrowing work listening to what people, sometimes from a very young age, had had to endure before somebody would listen to their story. I began to realise that I needed, while being totally open to hearing their stories, also not to fall into the grave mistake of condemning the abuser. The abuser too was a human being and in desperate need of help. To take sides would have been unethical and supremely unhelpful. I needed to find a heart wide enough to accept all beings, whatever their behaviour. The way forward was to find a balance between horrified condemnation and foolish acceptance of ghastly behaviour. We are not in control of the outcome and we try to do the best we can to resolve a bad situation for both sides. We can't back off saying it is beyond us to help. Help must be offered to all beings, however unconscionable their behaviour seems.

Looking into the harm blaming can lead to, it is useful to see how blame agitates the heart, keeps it contracted and often leads to despair. Rarely are words and acts of healing and forgiveness born of an agitated heart.

Compassion is not a magical device that can instantly dispel all suffering, yet to talk of the 'transfer of merit' as a way to manifest compassion, may indeed seem magical. Why? Because it is an offering from the mind of 'don't know', and that mind is one that defies our ordinary craving for logic. In offering merit we are asking for help for this *being*, or for this *situation*, without specifying the parameters of what that help should be. I don't find it difficult to set aside any notions of what form that help should take. The struggle for me is with the unanswerable question, of *who I am appealing to*. I can't seem to dodge this question by saying I am praying to the Buddhas and Ancestors. So all I can say for now, is that I am trusting in the love, wisdom and compassion of reality.

Practice

9.

Other treasured aspects of Practice

OTHER JEWELS OF PRACTICE, most of which involve relationships with others.

THE SANGHA TREASURE

'Student to Man Gong, Korean Zen Master:
Which is the most precious and important of the Three Jewels?
Man Gong replied:
Sangha'.

How fortunate we are to be training together in the O.B.C. Sangha. How fortunate we are to have spiritual friends with whom to walk the path, people we can trust and turn to when we imagine we have lost the thread of how to go on with training. Ultimately we make our own choices and decisions, but it is so valuable to have somebody else to take refuge in before we gallop down a cul-de-sac or behave un-preceptually.

I sometimes wonder how other members of the O.B.C. regard democracy, as it does seem to be taking a battering in our world. I don't know, largely because I don't ask as I do not wish to get drawn into a political argument that ends up causing division. In the O.B.C. we follow the practice of decision making by consensus, wherein each monk decides whether they can live with a proposal even if they don't necessarily agree with it. Respect is paid to seniority in his process, thus novices do not have a vote, but even so their opinions are valued and listened to. At the same time, novices are taught to bow to senior monks who have more experience of monastic life and what it entails.

In our Order we do have rules, but we don't regard our personal understanding of them as sacrosanct as there could always be other ways of interpreting them in order to continue living together with others in harmony and in Truth. A good starting point with decision making is to learn to regard rules without becoming attached to their particular form. This makes it easier to study them with increasing clarity and less emotionality. Then we can move with others towards a consensus of what is to be done that is genuinely 'good to do'. We find ourselves able and willing to release our personal views. In doing so we realise that 'right view' as described in the Precepts is essentially no view at all. How exciting and lively, practice within the Sangha can be!

The word 'freedom' may suggest that we can do anything we want, including acting unethically or destructively. But there is a more vital kind of freedom, one that proves to be more truly freeing; it is that if we follow trustworthy rules and ethics, we no longer need to think excessively or worry about our choice of action. Thus, we find a complete freedom *as a result* of rules and ethics.

Sangha has the role of teacher for it serves as a link to Buddha Nature and all the qualities we wish to exemplify. It is possible though, that if there is an exclusive focus on an individual teacher we may unnecessarily tie ourselves in knots. Rather then, let us accept the challenge to find the Middle Way between focusing on a particular individual as though they were the font of all knowledge, and at the other extreme of seeing only how much other Sangha members also teach. In accepting this challenge, we begin to realize that if we believe our teacher can do no wrong what can follow is that we end up believing that any disagreement with our teacher must be because we are deluded. Is that helpful? So the sangha jewel invites us to hold a paradox, and with it the struggle to find a path between making the teacher-disciple relationship too personal on the one hand, or too impersonal on the other. We humans are such binary creatures, we find paradoxes very disquieting and try to avoid them by insisting things are black or white.

Reflect on how you relate to your Sangha. How do you handle difficulties in sangha relationships, both difficulties which you are involved in and difficulties you observe between others? If such difficulties arise, step away at least until the situation has had time to lose some of its intense fire. It also helps if you can acknowledge any competitiveness within yourself, for then your appreciation of others can flourish and mutual inspiration is given a fertile field wherein to grow.

There is, and has surely always been a variety of perspectives in all monasteries from the very beginning, and some of them apparently contradictory. It must help to consider that own our view may be merely a preference, one option among many options. None of us is free from being blinded from time to time by our own view.

Happiness and suffering are not individual matters. The Sangha is in you and you are in the Sangha. We interpenetrate each other. Despite the costs, there were also benefits amongst the pain of the death of so many, and the isolation that so many experienced due to the Covid pandemic. The monastic Sangha at Throssel Hole Buddhist Abbey was offered the opportunity for deepening its Sangha building in a cohesive and loving way, even though it was at times difficult to grab this precious opportunity, particularly when fear was uppermost in people's hearts. It wasn't always easy for members of the community to look at each other with the eyes of equanimity and non-discrimination, but we began to see that being included in a Sangha does allow space for transformation to take place more quickly. We learnt to behave as one organism, and in doing so found the enormous benefits Sangha has to offer. Master Man Gong was onto something when he said the Sangha is the most precious and important of the Three Jewels.

How we behave as a Sangha is not only of value to us personally but to others. Here is an illustration from King

Prasenajit, who said to the Buddha; *'Dear teacher, every time I see your community of monks and nuns, I have great faith in you'*. Wouldn't it be wonderful if our behaviour as practitioners in the O.B.C. could inspire such faith in the Zen practice of *our* Order?

BALANCE AND EQUANIMITY

In training, finding balance and equanimity may well depend on the undivided wish to give whatever life asks, for *giving* is the real nature of life. If we regard life's unfolding as just the way life is, and don't label our own lives as hard or easy, we can be said to be living a balanced life. If balance and equanimity requires intense effort, something is out of kilter. Balance and equanimity is at the core of our being. So ask yourselves whether you are behaving in ways that prevent equanimity arising naturally. Encourage yourself to delve deeply into who and what you are. You can discover a core of balance, of stable energy, of equanimity, regardless of constantly changing circumstances. Then you can rest in the 'knowing' quality of the mind itself. No matter what comes and goes, this 'knowing' quality of mind remains. And hand in hand with this, there is the warm dark of uncertainty.

In 'The Scripture of Great Wisdom' we sing; *For here there is no suffering, nor yet again is there accumulation: Nor again annihilation nor an Eightfold Path, no knowledge, no attainment'*.

Look into the checkout person's eyes at the supermarket and see the universe looking back. What is this? For me this implies that uncertainty, or 'not knowing', is not to be dreaded, since it is the real state at that moment. Acknowledging 'not knowing' and not trying to hide from it allows any resources that I have, deeply ignorant as I am, to be part of reality. And I can 'know' these resources are enough.

As we recite in 'The Most Excellent Mirror–Samādhi'; *If there is no service, no advice. Such action and most unpretentious work all foolish seem and dull but those who practise thus this law continually shall in all worlds, be called Lord of Lords for eternity'.*

Facing some situation, or another being, or the catastrophe of our dying planet when I don't know how to react…I find this very, very unsettling. Then out of the blue help comes. For instance, I heard recently of the Nigerian poet Ben Okri's offering of a grass installation on the River Thames on which were these words:

> *'Can't you hear the future weeping?*
> *Our love must save the world.'*

I felt less dispirited and alone in the horror of what we are doing to our planet. Of course, I know it is not up to me alone, and I am flooded with gratitude for other people—people like David Attenborough and the Dalai Lama, who even in old age keep on pointing out uncomfortable truths about human behaviour. This I admire, and I wish I could be as wise and compassionate as them without blaming and condemning others. In the background of my past history are mistakes that make me squirm. There were times when I was opinionated and foolish about what needed changing in society, and took pride in being an anarchist, fighting for what I thought was right and just. It was the 'excitement' of the struggle that trapped me, rather than the ideals themselves.

FORTITUDE

Fortitude is the ability to remain calm when confronting harm and suffering. It is an antidote to unnecessary anger. We learn to act firmly, which in itself is sometimes a peaceful strength, at others an assertive compassion. I ask myself *who am I* in these changing circumstances. In part I am asking myself what my purpose in life is. We all can ask what our most deeply held values and concerns are. Another way of putting the question is; *why do we train?*

Surely it is a hiding to nothing to hope that by training we may become other than we are, for there is never any escape from ourselves. What we can rightly aim for is to be more present with the consequences, partly of our own making, that surround us in daily life. We then become at peace, content with being 'one with no name'. Wisdom is to be gained when we realise the inherent emptiness of existence; when we sense the truly empty nature of the self. This helps us to recognise the limits of our current understanding and to foster the humility to accept how little we know and how little we understand of the world. To do this we are required to relinquish the strutting ego, to ask it to quieten down and step out of the way of its attempt to prevent our awakened heart revealing itself. We become lighter, we can even laugh affectionately at our oh-so familiar foibles. Indeed, fear of them being revealed to others dissipates, and we welcome our mistakes being seen and being gently accepted by others, as it binds us together in our fallible humanness. Lighten up, and turn around well-established habits of striking out and blaming. Contact the kindness and compassion you already have, for they are not yours but the nature of the universe flowing through you.

BUDDHISM AND PSYCHOTHERAPY

I find myself from time to time being pushed yet again to ask if Buddhism and Psychotherapy are similar endeavours. I used to be a psychotherapist in what now feels like a long distant past life. My answer today would be that although both disciplines aim to transform the individual, their methods are strikingly different, as is the kind of transformation they seek. Psychotherapy aims to create a coherent sense of self. Buddhist psychology aims to transcend the self. So a successful outcome for most therapists is a person who is happy, relaxed, well-adjusted to their society, and able to function gracefully in their relationships. However, ask yourself if such a person is somebody you want to emulate. Those who have changed our world for the good have often not been well-adjusted to their society; rather they have kicked against it and stood out for a better world.

A successful outcome for a Buddhist practitioner can encompass many possibilities; the steady disciplined life of a lay practitioner, or of a monk living in a community with other monks, or on their own in a priory. However, there are also those who live the life of a hermit away from society, or a wild and crazy seeming person whose equanimity and compassion shines through their seemingly mad behaviour.

While therapist and client may agree to leave certain useful defences in place, on the spiritual path nothing is left unquestioned. The quest is for Truth; for Reality not happiness. Awakening is not about eliminating or devaluing the self; it is about letting go of identifying with the self, of losing the sense of self that is separate from the rest of the universe. This is what leads to freedom and peace of mind.

It is not that those who persevere with spiritual practice do not become aware of therapeutic consequences. Often, to our astonishment, we find we have become more loving, compassionate and equanimous. It may at first sight seem odd that letting go of desire, giving up your sense of self and what that self insists it needs, can possibly have such results.

Listen carefully—for we are not being asked to give up our sense of being a person who has something to offer others, and the world. However, it does mean we cannot continue to believe it is important to be a separate self who is in control of (at least) itself, and has free will to do what seems best. Here is a helpful quote from Reverend Daishin Morgan, in; 'Buddha Recognizes Buddha.' *'Self-restraint is not the tyranny that some suppose, and it is hard to see how one could come to any real sense of peace without it, and yet it must have its end. It is slowly overtaken by the undivided wish to give whatever life asks, because giving is the real nature of life, not restraint.'*

Here is another helpful quote, this time from Stephen Batchelor, in 'Buddhism without Beliefs'; *'The aim of dharma practice is to free ourselves from the illusion of freedom.'*

It may well be a foolish thing to embark on a search for spiritual transformation expecting it to make you happier. The search may make you feel happy at times, and then again it may well not—for chasing after happiness can get in the way of finding true satisfaction. For some the spiritual enterprise takes off where therapy ends. Perhaps for some of us psychotherapy is a way into embarking on the greater task of *seeing through* the self. That is to say, you have to be 'somebody', before you can be 'nobody'. Some say we have to learn to face crucial developmental life stages head-on instead of attempting to avoid them in the name of spirituality or enlightenment. This self-related task is for many of us important as a first step. Then we are better equipped to work on understanding the deeper reality; that the experience of being, or having, a *self* is a case of mistaken identity. It is in fact a misrepresentation born of anxiety and conflict about who we are. So this understanding is not a 'doing', but an 'undoing'; a giving up

80.

and an abandonment of the false belief that there is anyone here to abandon. What else is there to do!

Other treasured aspects of Practice

10.

Enlightenment...Awakening

BUDDHA NATURE INVITES US TO EXPLORE life in a new way; not with an eye to correcting what is wrong, rather with an eye to noticing what has, from the beginning, been right. A profound quality of Buddha Nature is awareness. It is the thread that runs through every experience. It runs through our constantly changing thoughts and emotions, nudging us to understand how they are influenced in turn by the changing conditions of our world and by the shifting perspectives our mind adopts. Awareness helps us understand how our reactions and perspectives come and go. Yet, despite these changes, awareness is always there; wide-open and accommodating like the sky, immeasurably deep like the ocean, and stable and enduring like a massive mountain. Awareness is whole and complete, always here. It can accommodate anything.

Awareness just is, it is not something we do. It is so close we often don't see it. We make awareness a problem when, for whatever reason, we can't believe it is there. This may be because of its effortless presence. 'Surely', we say to ourselves, 'we have to strive for awakening'. NO! Awakening is in the moment, it can never be yesterday's experience, but the realization of what is right now. We need to nourish bodhicitta, the mind that seeks the way of things as they actually are. The mind that naturally responds to the need of the moment, and does whatever is 'good to do'. Such a natural response will not tainted by the small self's longing for affirmation. We free ourselves from *trying* to be awakened, when we realize that we are already awakened. This does not mean however, that there isn't still practice to be done.

Dōgen says in 'Bendōwa', or 'On the endeavor of the Way' (from the 'Shōbōgenzō'); *When even for a moment you sit upright in samādhi expressing the Buddha mudra in the three activities (body, speech and thought), the whole world of phenomena becomes the Buddha's mudra and the entire sky turns into enlightenment'.*

When I try to recognize awareness it helps to choose to study the internal and external environment of this Leandra-being. I know the most reliable data comes when there is an attitude or intentional stance of non-attached equanimity, for then it is less likely to be being skewed by greed, anger and delusion. Every moment of awareness is often distorted by an emotional response, thus it requires a thoroughgoing equanimity. This does not mean you don't care or are indifferent. This equanimity is evenly balanced and fully aware of things exactly as they are, without desiring to change them or preferring one state to another.

I begin to wonder if it is actually helpful to say intentional awareness means paying attention to the present moment. For what really is the present moment? Mental objects like thoughts occur in the present moment even when their content is taken from past or future. When we talk of being aware in the present moment, what is needed is to be aware of the act of thinking without getting caught up in the content of those thoughts. Intentional awareness seems to require being engaged with the object of our attention, but disengaged from craving; thus preceptual action is given space to flourish. Although attention, volition and concentration are needed to assist us in behaving benevolently, they are also brought into play when we misbehave and act non-preceptually. There is a subtlety here which may seem paradoxical.

The more alert we are to the shifts in what we see, hear and feel, the more we allow thoughts and feelings to be seen clearly, and this in turn encourages our thoughts and feelings to dissolve. When we are simply present with what is happening within and around us, love and compassion naturally emerge. Like awareness they are not qualities we have to develop or cultivate for they are abiding qualities of our Buddha Nature. Love, wisdom, compassion and awareness are our Buddha Nature. However, if we just sit back and do nothing, nothing will change. What a paradox! The key to unlocking this paradox is recognition. Buddha Nature is not something we do, it is something within us to recognise. Such recognition opens that ever-present spaciousness to be seen and felt, and thus brings the wisdom into view that keeps us from getting lost in immediate reactivity.

So what is it like to be you now? Open your mind a little to watch your own awareness. Scrutinize as carefully as you can.

What is it really like? Undoubtedly, there is something that it is like to be you now. If watching intently, you will see that what you imagine you are keeps changing. It is difficult enough to say in words what exactly it is like to be you in the flow of change. If you start wondering what it is like to be somebody else, or some other aspect of the world, it gets even more complicated. And we *are* interested in other things, other beings, and what makes them tick. This is what draws some extraordinary people to be willing to offer themselves and their lives to other beings, and to the whole world.

Susan Blackmore writes in her book 'Consciousness – an introduction': *The cognitive scientist Stephen Pinker has suggested that we can still get on with the job of understanding how the mind works, but our awareness is 'the ultimate tease...forever beyond our intellectual grasp'.*

Awareness though, is the fundamental nature of our mind. It is beyond suffering and pain, beyond life and death. We must always allow awareness to extend beyond any particular experience, because awareness cannot be limited, or destroyed, or stopped. It is the Unborn. This is our true nature, our Buddha Nature, the ultimate refuge and reality itself.

WAKING UP

Buddha urged people not to be satisfied with hearsay or tradition, but to look within to see the truth. It is said that his last words were; *'Work out your own salvation with diligence'*. Each of us needs to ask ourselves if we are stuck with the problems and illusions we have unearthed, or if we are learning to see through them. The Buddha was a human being, and his great gift to us is the example of how a person can wake up from the dream of being a separate self.

I have found these words of Stephen Batchelor to be helpful; *The four noble truths are not propositions to be believed in but truths to be acted on. An inquiry into oneself that supposedly reveals the emptiness and impermanence of all phenomena, the illusory nature of self, and the origins and nature of suffering.'* (From 'Buddhism without beliefs').

Waking up is often described as though it were the endpoint of a long journey on a spiritual path. But some people claim that they just 'woke up' and that their awakening was the beginning, rather than the culmination of their spiritual life. Awakening might well turn out to be not the culmination of a journey, but the realisation instead that we never left our spiritual home in the first place. As in fact nobody can, for Buddha Nature is the fundamental nature of our mind. It is beyond suffering and pain, beyond life and death. It is vital to see that Buddha Nature, just like awareness, extends beyond any particular experience.

Someone once asked if the experience of enlightenment is some kind of an accident and meditation just helps us become more accident-prone. Others ask if the experience of enlightenment is a consequence of past lives. I guess that each of us at some point can have different ideas about how enlightenment comes about. The idea of past lives, in particular can be a very attractive one, after all, it is so tempting to make up a story about a past life that explains our behaviour in this life. But do we really know what happened in a life before this one? We should investigate the possibility that we are creating a pleasing, soothing fantasy that explains our current difficulties. While in Buddhism there is the notion of the wheel of death and rebirth as a graphic explanation of the constant re-creation of new 'selves' moment-to-moment from the prevailing conditions, yet it is only too easy to fall into the trap of mistaking the re-creation of new selves as evidence of a continuing 'self', and that would be a mistake.

Some of us may inadvertently choose to manufacture problems for ourselves by ignoring, or refusing to acknowledge, our longing that this 'self' be permanent and survive our seeming death. You could try saying again and again; 'I don't know what death brings', so that you are less likely to fall entirely into the enchanted spell of your own standpoint. Check that such a standpoint has not been arrived at in the first place just because of your longing that your darkest and most fearful wishes should not come true.

KENSHO

For me, as the life of training has unfolded, what some may describe as kensho has been no more than a temporary experience of what I might call enlightenment. I would describe such experiences as tiny glimpses of a profound sense of opening to something greater. Teachers wisely tend to be sceptical and prod the trainee who tells them about their kensho. They don't necessarily take such self-reports at face value. Wise teachers measure what the student reports within the history and the trajectory of the student's life of practice, and the manner in which the report is given. Observation of daily practice is very useful for the teacher to assess the student. It also, conversely, offers an opportunity for the teacher to learn from the student. Such a circular flow of learning is wonderful and humbling. Dōgen describes it as the circle of the Way.

The matter of ultimate enlightenment, or of full awakening needs probing into, for what does this mean if, as Dōgen says, we are inherently enlightened from the start? Dōgen's question was if we are enlightened from the beginning why is training necessary? As we recite in 'Rules for Meditation', *Why are training and enlightenment differentiated since the Truth is Universal? Since Truth is not separate from training, training is unnecessary'.*

Thus far, all I can honestly come up with is that enlightenment is not a 'state' at all. Everything, absolutely everything, is just the same as it always was, because everything is inherently enlightened. It cannot be explained, or described.

Anything you may try to say is beside the point. Yet, paradoxically one person can do things, or point to things, to help another realise enlightenment and in this way we could say enlightenment is passed on. It seems to require deep questioning of both self and other to come to what enlightenment really means. Sometimes it is described as transmission outside the scriptures. And then again I wonder if enlightenment is more to do with losing, not gaining, for it requires the willingness to let go, and to drop everything before one can see through illusions. It is definitely possible to stand free of the juggernaut of 'self', even if only for moments at a time.

Then there is simply the saying attributed to Layman Pang; *Before enlightenment chop wood, carry water. After enlightenment chop wood, carry water'.*

CONDITIONED ARISING - CO-DEPENDENT ORIGINATION

Buddha taught that all things are relative and interdependent, arising out of what came before and in turn giving rise to something else, in a vast web of causes and effects. To others you may simply be a person *in the world*, but what I find shines a light on co-dependent arising, is the possibility that I am simultaneously a space *in which* the world happens. Those practising within any tradition will inevitably be influenced by their teachers, thus the effects, for instance of meditation on the student may be heavily dependent on the expectations they carry with them, taken in turn from what they believed the teacher was pointing to. So I ask myself how much my Master has influenced me, and whether in my love and respect for him, I have ever found it too hard sometimes to question his teaching. If I could never question my teacher's teaching, how then could I give myself permission to do what ultimately we all need to do, which is to find our own way, rather than so diligently modelling ourselves on our teachers that we become clones. As the Buddha said; *'Work out your own salvation with diligence'.* I try to take this to heart.

REAL MIND

The Indian monk Bodhidharma and Emperor Wu met when Bodhidharma first arrived in China. The Emperor was a devout Buddhist intent on gaining merit through good works and he asked Bodhidharma how much merit he had gained. Bodhidharma replied; *'None whatsoever'.*

This is a vital teaching for all of us to digest. All deeds are empty not because they are devoid of meaning, but because nothing is fixed and separate. A teacher can see to some extent into a questioner's mind and then leave them slithering around. Though very disconcerting, the student is in the end grateful for the teacher's percipience.

Here is more of the dialogue between Emperor Wu and Bodhidharma:

'Emperor Wu: What is real mind?
Bodhidharma: When pure wisdom is complete, the essence is empty and serene. Such mind cannot be attained through worldly activity.
Emperor Wu: What is foremost sacred truth?
Bodhidharma: Vast emptiness, nothing sacred.
Emperor Wu: What is it that faces me?
Bodhidharma: I don't know.'

Bodhidharma's provocative replies challenge all of us to let go of consoling beliefs, and dwell in the unknowing perplexity of emptiness. Some days this can feel more challenging than I can bear, and I long for what Keats described as; *'easeful death'*. It helps me to remember that this is familiar territory and I am encouraged once again to stop trying to dodge pain and uncertainty. Rather, it is for me to sit as still as I can for as long is necessary with what can seem to be unbearable feelings and thoughts.

The helpful memory comes to me of a winter three month retreat at the hermitage in Wales. I did not turn to my Master for help during this time. I still don't completely understand why, and I wonder if it was a sort of obstinacy that was manifesting, or a sense that ultimately I had to find my own way without expecting another to keep pointing it out to me. It was, as it were time to become a spiritual adult. Somehow though my Master, Reverend Master Daishin must have sensed the struggle I was having, because he sent an encouraging card to me about finding a way in the echo chamber of the mind. This helped me to investigate the nature of my immediate experiences, and to dare to question why I was training.

I needed to ask myself what I was hoping to gain and whether monasticism was really the path for me. I wondered whether if I returned to lay life the pain and confusion would dissipate. But I knew in my bones this was not the answer. Thus I tried another tack, and that was when I was drawn to reread Keats 'Ode to a Nightingale', wherein he described himself as being half in love with easeful death.

THE VIEW FROM WITHIN

Let us try looking into our own minds, or rather, as Zazen guides us, to not so much 'look', so much as to 'watch', which is less deliberate and more trusting. During meditation, we can be completely free from the chain of causation. It is a state in which we can be anybody and anywhere. We are what we meditate. We are also the source of cause and effect. A question may arise of who is looking into what. Yet looking itself changes what is seen. The experience may seem 'ineffable', too great or extreme to be expressed in words; too sacred to be uttered, and then we are left alone with it. Don't despair though. Don't give up. Keep asking questions. Don't shrink away from the challenge. Questioning yourself is extremely helpful and the answers interesting, so allow them to keep coming. Even when you feel you can't share your questions with others because you don't even know how to articulate them for yourself, don't give up. A question already contains the answer. Trust yourself and your training.

I have found a type of temporary comfort which gives me the breathing space to regroup, and then to try again. I look out of the window at the garden. I take it all in with a single gulp and then try to describe the things in the garden, giving names to all the different objects. For instance, naming the shrubs and trees, how many are there? Watching the small birds feeding, I try naming them. Seeing larger birds flying overhead to different destinations though, I have noticed that in accessing some parts of my experience, others disappear or become unavailable. This simple exercise in consciousness encourages me to keep questioning.

I am in better shape to consider what Shunryu Suzuki meant in 'Zen mind, Beginner's mind', when he said; '*Nothing comes from outside your mind*'. For me this implies that my mind—the view from within—already includes reality, it includes everything. Reality does not come from outside my mind. This leads on to asking myself to consider whether on occasion I am unnecessarily making waves in my mind. The beauty of accepting this, is that if you leave mind as it is, it will become calm and limitlessly spacious. This mind is real mind. Don't be concerned that if you drop the intellectual thinking you are giving up. Rather, consider the worth of the intellect. Avoid making a division between the spiritual and the intellectual. In real mind there must be room for both. Ask yourself if the root of any disquiet might be that you are bothered by your thinking.

When Tibetan Buddhists speak of real, or big mind they often point to their chests, not their heads, for the brain is seen as merely the thinking mind. Big mind is how they define reality, a direct knowing of reality which is basically open and friendly to what is. This openness is the central feature of human consciousness. An awakened heart allows a complete attunement with reality. It encourages a capacity to touch and be touched, a capacity to reach out and let in. A swinging door that opens in both directions.

We refer to this capacity when we use verbal expressions such as; 'my heart went out to them', or 'I took her to my heart'. What shuts down the heart reaching out, is our not letting ourselves be confident of our own experience. We are so quick to judge and to criticise ourselves. This judgmental attitude may be fuelled by trying to express what we know in a way we think others may find acceptable. We need to have the courage to 'show' ourselves, and in our yearning to be authentic, to be prepared for the troublesome questions to arise again: What, or who am I? What is the point of it all? To wonder even, if such questions will forever be unanswerable, for in myself I find however deeply I try to explore the terrain I never seem able to reach the real depth.

EMPTINESS

If you look closely enough, letting go of all preconceptions, subject and objects disappear into a cloud. Watching closely, that cloud disappears into a bigger cloud. The result is that there is nothing substantial anywhere. The only real thing is connection: void touching void.

This is described in 'The Scripture of Great Wisdom', (paraphrased); *no suffering, no accumulation, no annihilation, no Eightfold Path, no knowledge, no attainment...going on beyond this human mind.*

Yet appearances remain valid as appearances. There is no reality beyond appearances other than the emptiness of every appearance. So there is nothing to argue for, or against. In being empty, everything is free of argument; lighter than air. Assistance in understanding this comes when there is knowing that whatever happens is just what happens, there is no need for us to get tangled up with the whys and wherefores. Saying that *phenomena have no intrinsic existence* does not mean they don't exist but that they don't exist as we think they do. That is to say, they don't exist as freestanding, independent, solid and real entities. Everything is contingent, not set in stone; rather it ceases simultaneously with the moment it arises.

When you meditate something always happens; maybe you can't identify it, or you barely notice it, but something does happen. It always happens wherever you are, however brief the stillness. There is an experience. There is a faint glimmer that the world you have always assumed to be the world; the only world; the whole world and nothing but the world, may not be as you have assumed it to be. Your Mind, your Self, may not be as they have seemed to you in the past. I am encouraging you to take on board an appreciation of emptiness that you may have missed because you have defined it as an appreciation beyond the capability of somebody as ordinary of yourself; an appreciation only reached by deeply spiritual beings. But it is not as rare and as out of reach as you thought; it is actually rather common.

However, do not flip to the other extreme, for as Great Master Dōgen says, in 'Rules for Meditation', (with Reverend Master Jiyu's emphasis); *'WHEN THE OPPOSITES ARISE, THE BUDDHA MIND IS LOST'.* He continues: *'However much you may be proud of your understanding, however much you may be enlightened, whatever your attainment of wisdom and supernatural power, your finding of the way to mind illumination, your power to touch heaven and enter into enlightenment, when the opposites arise you have almost lost the way to salvation.'*

The more you meditate the more emptiness is experienced. You could describe your sitting as; training yourself in knowing emptiness, or as; training yourself to let go of the frightened, greedy, deluded small, small self. As you will begin to understand that all phenomena, though empty, are marvellous, connected, and magical; let us all awaken to the connectedness and indescribable meaning that is, and has always been our real life.

WHAT ARE YOU?

Let's start from a simple, straight-forward question. How comfortable are you in your own skin and with your own spirituality? It can be demanding to authentically be who we are, to stand firmly on the ground of what we do with our life in this multifaceted world. I have found I have been tempted to try to follow what I imagine my teacher is wanting me to understand without questioning their words. Is that because I do so wish to be accepted and to be regarded as a good O.B.C. trainee? Surely the 'squirrelyness' of this won't do. Surely I need to find my true sitting place, and not be overly influenced by the wish to please. Aren't we called on to respect ourselves as well as to respect others and to be willing to change, or to adapt in skillful and true ways? Aren't we called on to learn to really listen to dissenting voices in any discussion? A group may well come up with a better solution to a problem, than any individual who is apparently wanting their own way to be accepted by all as the best way forward. Keep in mind that a prejudicial view of one person can spread out and affect others.

PARADOX

Paradox presents a faithful picture of the fullness of life, so appreciate it as a means to spiritual growth. As the psychoanalyst C.G. Jung suggested; *paradox widens consciousness beyond the narrow*

Birth and Death

confines of a tyrannical intellect and thus allows the expression of transcendental truth.

Kōans are an excellent means for inviting paradox into your practice. Their seemingly impossible questions hold out the very means of wisely walking the path. While the Sōtō Zen tradition does not use kōans in quite the same way they do in Rinzai Zen, all kōans have their origins in conversations between people interested in the unravelling of the twists and turns of human life. Perhaps that is why one of these kōans may at times beckon to you for your attention, and yet, at the same time we are encouraged to realise that, in a very personal way; *'the kōan arises naturally in daily life'*, ('Rules for Meditation').

Because of a renewed interest in the teaching of Bodhidharma I often find myself asking; *'what is merit?'* Bodhidharma's answer to Emperor Wu; *'No merit at all'* feels right on the money for me, especially when I have done something useful. Yet it also feels right when I have made another bumbling mistake. Whatever the reason, there is a nagging sense that I still haven't penetrated the kōan of 'no merit' at all.

Also, when asking *'what am I?'* my heart resonates with Bodhidharma's answer to the Emperor's question; *'Who is it that stands before me?'* Bodhidharma, of course answered; *'I don't know'.* When I ask myself *'what am I',* or more impersonally; *'what is this?'* my answer inevitably is; *'I don't know'.* All I am certain of, is that I am required to toss overboard any answers I have come up with, and anything I have imagined. Doing so, I begin to sense a sturdy link to enlightenment that such questioning demands. I know I must step out of the way, so that a profound change of heart can enable the world to be a different place; a different place where joy and kindness are more clearly apparent.

Kōans are not prescriptions for a better life; they are thorns in the flesh that provoke us to find our own particular way, a way suitable for our circumstances and our personalities. They provoke us to lead the best of lives possible and to offer our all to others. The unpredictability of life, which kōans point to is perhaps—to our bewildered surprise—beautiful and glorious. So how can we be churlish enough to ignore this and turn away? Instead, let us salute the adventure of life, let us write poetry, make art or otherwise invite creativity into our lives. Let us take a creative leap into the indescribable. Pablo Neruda wrote; *'Poetry arrived in search of me. I don't know, I don't know where it came from,'* (from a poem called 'Poetry').

Encourage doubt and uncertainty through finding the still centre of lifedeath, deathlife. The Sōtō Zen priest, Kōshō Uchiyama wrote;

> *'At the end of aging*
> *We can see that*
> *Lifedeath is one Life*
> *Not life and death*
> *Lifedeath is undivided'*

Step into the vast, vast field of uncertainty where you will find the Way waiting patiently for your arrival. So what if you die! Of course we all are going to die, and if we do not deny death we can truly and vividly live our lives. Doing so, we are outwitting any fear of death. Our lives will be strong and vital, not dependent on our physical or any other condition. What delight is found in adapting to all conditions, whether personal or of the world around us. Discrimination between 'want' and 'don't want', or 'good' and 'bad' dissolve of themselves; then the paper walls of our cell of fear tear apart, and happiness arrives for no good reason, seemingly uninvited.

Curiosity reveals the secrets of a life worth living.

Enlightenment...Awakening

About the Author

Reverend Master Leandra Robertshaw was ordained in 1998, and is a disciple of Reverend Master Daishin Morgan, previously the Abbot of Throssel Hole Buddhist Abbey.

She is a mother and a grandmother, and now herself, since 2019 the Abbot of the monastery in which she serves.

Notes